Corporate Acquisitions and Mergers in Croatia

Andrijana Kaštelan

This book was originally published as a chapter in Corporate Acquisitions and Mergers.

General Editor: Peter Begg

Wolters Kluwer

Published by:
Kluwer Law International B.V.
PO Box 316
2400 AH Alphen aan den Rijn
The Netherlands
E-mail: lrs-sales@wolterskluwer.com
Website: www.wolterskluwer.com/en/solutions/kluwerlawinternational

Sold and distributed by:
Wolters Kluwer Legal & Regulatory U.S.
920 Links Avenue
Landisville, PA 17538
United States of America
E-mail: customer.service@wolterskluwer.com

ISBN 978-94-035-0037-9

e-Book: ISBN 978-94-035-0047-8
web-PDF: ISBN 978-94-035-0057-7

Contents

Kinstellar ... xi

1 Local Economic, Political and Cultural Aspects ... 1
 1.1 General Comments on the Country Profile ... 1
 1.2 Historical Background ... 1
 1.3 Legal System ... 2
 1.4 Cultural Aspects ... 3

2 The Regulatory Framework ... 3
 2.1 Companies Act ... 3
 2.2 Available Corporate Structures ... 4
 2.3 Commercial Register ... 4
 2.4 Data Mailboxes ... 5
 2.5 Common Transactions ... 5
 2.6 Comparison of Limited Liability Company and Joint-Stock Company ... 6
 2.7 Ultimate Beneficial Owners Registry ... 16

3 Laws Affecting M&A ... 17
 3.1 Regulatory Framework ... 17

4 Transformations ... 18
 4.1 General Framework ... 18
 4.2 Mergers ... 18
  4.2.1 Merger by Acquisition ... 18
  4.2.2 Merger by Consolidation ... 18
 4.3 Cross-Border Transformations ... 19
 4.4 Demerger ... 19
 4.5 Transformation of a Legal Form ... 19

5 Relevant Regulatory Authorities ... 20

6 Controls/Restrictions on Foreign Investment ... 21
 6.1 Acquisition of Real Estate by Foreigners ... 21

7 Acquisition of Regulated Entities ... 21
 7.1 Banks ... 21
 7.2 Investment Firms ... 22
 7.3 Central Securities Depository and Organizers of Regulated Markets ... 22
 7.4 Management Companies and Investment Funds ... 23
 7.5 Pension Companies Managing Obligatory Pension Funds ... 23

7.6 Pension Companies Managing Voluntary Pension Funds 24
7.7 Insurance/Reinsurance Companies 24
7.8 Credit Unions 24
7.9 Payment Institutions 24
7.10 Other Specific Industries 25

8 Incentives for Foreign Investment 25
8.1 General Information 25
8.2 Current Forms of Investment Incentives 25
8.3 Competent investment authority 25

9 Specific Issues of Company/Securities Law 26
9.1 Financial Assistance 26
9.2 Security Interests 26
9.3 Completion Formalities 27

10 Insolvency 29
10.1 General 29
10.2 Pre-bankruptcy 30
10.3 Bankruptcy 31
10.3.1 Effects of Commencing Insolvency Proceedings, Decision on Insolvency and Declaration of Bankruptcy 31
10.3.2 Avoidance Actinos – Claims of Preference or Creditor Prejudice 32
10.3.3 The Bankruptcy Trustee 34
10.3.4 The Court (*dodao sam ovaj dio o sudu, činilo mi se bitnim*) 35
10.3.5 Creditors' Committee 36
10.3.6 Creditors' Assembly 36
10.3.7 Distribution of Assets: Priority Claims and Ranking 36

11 Choice of Law 38
11.1 Choice of Law 38
11.2 Jurisdiction 38
11.3 Arbitration 39

12 Most Common Acquisition Transactions 39
12.1 Types of Transactions 39
12.2 General Information 39
12.3 Transfer of Liabilities 40
12.4 Representations and Warranties 40
12.5 Acquisition of Shares in a Joint-stock Company 40
12.5.1 Transfer of Shares 40

12.5.2 Consequences of the Acquisition of Shares 41
12.5.3 Issues to Be Considered in Share Deals 42
12.5.4 Squeeze-Out with Transfer of Shares to the Majority Shareholder 42
12.6 Acquisition of an Ownership Interest in a Limited Liability Company 43
12.7 Acquisition of Assets 44
12.7.1 General 44
12.7.2 Specification of Assets and Liabilities 44
12.7.3 Acquired Liabilities 44

13 Specific Rules on Public Takeovers 45
13.1 General 45
13.2 Obligation to Publish Takeover Bid 45
13.3 Financial Aspects 46
13.4 Duties of the Board of Directors 46

14 Other Relevant Laws, Anti-bribery 46
14.1 Anti-bribery Laws 46
14.2 Act on the Criminal Liability of Legal Entities 47
14.2.1 General Information 47
14.2.2 'Attributability' of Acts Committed by Certain Individuals to a Legal Entity 48
14.2.3 Exemption from Punishment 48
14.2.4 Succession of Criminal Liability to Legal Successors 48
14.2.5 Sanctions 48
14.2.6 Enforcement Trends 48
14.3 Money-laundering Regulations 48

15 The Due Diligence Process 49
15.1 General Introduction 49
15.2 Specific Issues to Be Reviewed 51
15.3 Disclosure Restrictions 52
15.3.1 General 52
15.3.2 Business Secrets 52
15.3.3 Personal Data Protection 53
15.3.4 Banking Secrets 53
15.3.5 Other Restrictions 54

16 Role of the Courts 55
16.1 General 55
16.2 Court System 56
16.3 Costs and Timing 57
16.4 Enforceability of Key Contractual Provisions 58
16.4.1 Restrictive Covenants 59

16.4.2 Confidentiality Constraints 60
16.4.3 Protection of Minority Shareholder Rights 60
16.4.4 Enforcement of Warranty and Indemnity Claims 61

17 Other Dispute Resolution Mechanisms 62
17.1 Arbitration 62
17.2 Mediation 62

18 Merger Control/Competition Law Issues 63
18.1 General Introduction 63
18.2 Merger Control Test 63
18.2.1 Concentration 64
18.2.2 Turnover Thresholds 65
18.2.3 Transaction Subject to European Merger Control 65
18.3 Notification Procedure 65
18.3.1 Notifying Party 65
18.3.2 Commencement of the Merger Proceedings 66
18.3.3 Notification 66
18.3.4 Stages of the Proceedings 68
18.4 Implementation of the Transaction 69
18.4.1 Mandatory Suspension of Implementation 69
18.4.2 Application for an Exemption 69
18.4.3 Consequences 70
18.5 Competition Authority's Authorizations 70
18.5.1 Right to Information 70
18.5.2 Power to Investigate 70
18.6 Fines and Remedial Measures 70
18.6.1 Fines 70
18.6.2 Remedial Measures 71

19 Taxation Aspects 71
19.1 Nature of the Tax Regime 71
19.2 Liability to Tax 71
19.2.1 Corporate Tax Rate 72
19.2.2 Taxes on Capital Gains 72
19.2.3 CFC Rules 73
19.2.4 Value Added Tax or Sales Taxes or Other Taxes on Revenue/Sales 73
19.2.5 Stamp Duties or Other Taxes on Land Transactions 74
19.2.6 Other Taxes on Land or Real Estate 74

19.2.7 Capital Duties or Other Duties on Share Capital 74
19.2.8 Business Rates 74
19.2.9 Taxes Imposed on Employers (For Example, PAYE and Social Security Obligations) 74
19.2.10 Customs and Excise Duties 75
19.2.11 R&D Costs 75
19.2.12 Exit tax 75
19.3 Tax Consolidation. Group Relief of Gains and Losses 75
19.4 Tax Considerations Arising on M&A Transactions 75
19.4.1 Transfer Taxes 76
19.4.2 Transfer of Tax Liabilities 76
19.4.3 Real Estate Transfer Tax 76
19.4.4 VAT 77
19.4.5 Transfer of Tax Liabilities 77
19.5 Structuring the Investment: Withholding Taxes 78
19.5.1 Dividends Paid to Foreign Corporate/ Group Shareholders 78
19.5.2 Dividends Paid to Foreign Individual Shareholders 78
19.5.3 Dividends Received from Foreign Subsidiaries/Affiliates 78
19.5.4 Interest Paid to Foreign Corporate/Group Shareholders or Affiliates 79
19.5.5 Interest Received from Foreign Corporate/ Group Shareholders or Affiliates 79
19.5.6 Intellectual Property (IP) Royalties Paid to Foreign Corporate/Group Shareholders or Affiliates 80
19.5.7 Intellectual Property (IP) Royalties Received from Foreign Corporate/Group Shareholders or Affiliates 80
19.5.8 Management or Consultancy Fees Paid to Foreign Corporate/Group Shareholders or Affiliates 80
19.5.9 Payments to Non-residents in Respect of the Purchase or Renting of Immovable Property 80
19.5.10 Double Tax Treaties 80
19.6 Debt Financing 81
19.6.1 Are Finance Costs Associated with the Acquisition Generally Deductible 81
19.6.2 Deductibility of Exceeding Borrowing Costs 81
19.7 Thin Capitalization 81

19.8 Transfer Pricing 81

20 Employment Considerations 82
20.1 General Introduction 82
20.2 Employment Contracts 82
20.2.1 General Concept 82
20.2.2 Obligatory Contents 82
20.3 Non-competition 83
20.3.1 Non-competition During Employment 83
20.3.2 Non-competition after Termination of Employment 84
20.4 Fixed-term Employment Contracts 84
20.4.1 Restrictions 84
20.4.2 Consequences 85
20.5 Employment of Top-level Managers 85
20.5.1 Defining a Top-Level Manager 85
20.5.2 Dismissal or Resignation of Top-Level Managers 85
20.6 Termination of the Employment Contract 85
20.6.1 Termination by Agreement 86
20.6.2 Termination by Notice 86
20.6.3 Immediate Cancellation 88
20.6.4 Collective Dismissal 88
20.6.5 Participation of Employee Council or Trade Unions in Termination of Employment 89
20.6.6 Severance Payment 89
20.7 Employment Representatives 90
20.7.1 Trade Unions 90
20.7.2 Employee Councils 90
20.7.3 Role of Employee Representatives 91
20.7.4 Collective Bargaining/Collective Agreements 91
20.7.5 Obligation to inform 92
20.7.6 Right of Consultation 92
20.7.7 Right to Decide Jointly 93
20.7.8 Right to Decide 93
20.8 Particular Aspects Related to Acquisitions 94
20.8.1 Share Transaction 94
20.8.2 Asset Transaction 94
20.9 Employment of Foreigners in Croatia 94
20.9.1 Employment by Local Entity 95
20.9.2 Secondment of an Employee to Croatia 95

21 Intellectual Property Rights 95
21.1 Copyright 95
21.1.1 Copyrighted Works 95
21.1.2 Authorship 96

21.1.3 Author's rights ... 96
21.1.4 Protection and Enforcement of Copyright ... 97
21.1.5 Due Diligence Verification ... 97

22 Industrial Property Rights ... 98
22.1 Registration of Industrial Property Rights ... 98
22.2 Protection and Enforcement of Industrial Property Rights ... 99
22.3 Due Diligence Verification ... 99

23 Accounting Treatment ... 99
23.1 General ... 99
23.2 Merger, Demerger, Squeeze-Out ... 100
23.3 Transformation of the Legal Form ... 100
23.4 Other Issues ... 100

KINSTELLAR

Kinstellar is an independent regional law firm in Emerging Europe and Central Asia, founded in 2008 as a spin-off of the Bratislava, Bucharest, Budapest and Prague offices of Linklaters. Since its foundation in 2008, Kinstellar has opened new offices in Istanbul (Turkey), Belgrade (Serbia), Bulgaria (Sofia), and Almaty (Kazakhstan), Uzbekistan (Tashkent) and Croatia (Zagreb). Kinstellar advises leading global and local companies, financial institutions and governments on their most challenging transactions and assignments.

Kinstellar's Zagreb office was established in 1995 under the name Žurić i Partneri under which it still operates in Croatia due to the Croatian Bar regulations. Having served international and local clients in all areas of business in Croatia for over twenty-five years, Žurić i Partneri Kinstellar is recognized as one of the most reputed law firms in Croatia.

This country chapter on Corporate M&A in the Republic of Croatia has been prepared by the following lawyers of Žurić i Partneri Kinstellar Zagreb: Edin Karakaš (Partner), Daniela Mayer (Counsel), Andrijana Kaštelan (Managing Associate), Vedran Kopilović (Managing Associate), Andrej Skljarov (Senior Associate), Tena Pajalić (Associate), Hrvoje Klišanić (Associate), Zrinka Ivanković (Associate), Kristina Marinov (Associate), and Luka Banožić (Junior Associate).

The country chapter has been reviewed and coordinated by Edin Karakaš (Partner), Andrijana Kaštelan (Managing Associate), and Petr Měšťánek, the Head of Know-how.

Žurić i Partneri Kinstellar
Savska cesta 32
10 000 Zagreb
Croatia
Tel.: (385) 1 5555 630
www.kinstellar.com

Disclaimer

This document does not purport to contain a comprehensive summary of all the legal risks and issues in the legal areas it covers. It is to be used for information only and cannot be relied upon as legal advice; no legal or business decision should be based solely on this document.

1 LOCAL ECONOMIC, POLITICAL AND CULTURAL ASPECTS

1.1 General Comments on the Country Profile

[01] Croatia is a country situated in Central Europe and South-East Europe. Due to its position, it was historically under the influence of the Austro-Hungarian Empire, Venice/Italy and the Ottoman Empire. It has a land surface area of 56 594 km^2 and is shaped as a crescent. Its neighbours are Slovenia to the west, Bosnia and Hercegovina within the crescent, Hungary to the North, Serbia to the north-east and Montenegro to the south-east. Croatia has a long sea border with Italy, but there is no direct land contact. The total population of Croatia is about 3 900 000 people. The capital city of Croatia is Zagreb, with a population of about 800 000 people.

[02] The official language of Croatia is Croatian, and the currency as of 1 January 2023 is the Euro, which replaced the Croatia kuna (HRK) as the national currency.

[03] The road network in Croatia is approximately 27 000 kilometres long, with 1.416 5 kilometres of motorways. The railway network is 2617 kilometres long. The country's main international airport is Franjo Tuđman in Zagreb. Other airports providing international air services are Split, Dubrovnik, Zadar, Rijeka, Pula and Osijek airports, and two island airports – on Brač and Mali Lošinj.

[04] One of the main attractions of the Croatian economy is its skilled and well-educated workers, who can be employed for considerably lower costs than those in western economies. Average gross monthly income was HRK 10.301 (approx. EUR1 370) in 2022.

[05] The Croatian economy is service-oriented, with tourism as the main sector of the economy. Tourism is centred around the Adriatic coast: Croatia has the largest charter fleet in the world. The food industry and ICT sectors also contribute significantly to the Croatian economy. While it does possess fertile land and rich agricultural resources, it does not have large quantities of mineral resources. There are significant sources of non-metal minerals used in the construction industry. Croatia has its own energy sources, including oil and gas, but is not self-sufficient in these. Croatia has great potential for renewable energy resources – wind, sun, hydro, biomass and geothermal energy. Croatia boasts a liquefied natural gas regasification terminal on the island of Krk, making it a potential gas hub for central and eastern Europe.

1.2 Historical Background

[06] The Croatian state was formed sometime in the ninth century. Since the early twelfth century, Croatia had been in a personal union with Hungary, where it remained until 1918. Being at the crossroads of Western and Eastern Europe, Croatian lands have historically been divided between the Kingdom of Croatia (as a part of the Croatian and Hungarian kingdom), and later the Austrian Empire, the Ottoman Empire and the Republic of Venice and, later, Italy. That division has had a significant impact on the language and culture of different parts of Croatia, but also on their legal tradition and administrative affairs – for example, land ownership in parts governed by these three powers was differently administered. From 1918 to 1991 Croatia was a part of a union of south Slavic nations called Yugoslavia – first as a kingdom under the rule of a Serbian dynasty, and from 1945 as a socialist federative republic led by a leader of the World War II anti-fascist movement, Josip Broz TIto. Between 1945 and 1991 Yugoslavia was neither a part of the North Atlantic Treaty Organization (NATO) nor of the Warsaw pact, but was rather a part of a Non-aligned Movement. While Yugoslavia had a one-party political system, it was comparatively free when compared to Warsaw Pact members. Similarly, it's economic system was not that of a communist country but embraced market-based socialism.

[07] Following Tito's death the Yugoslav economy started collapsing, leading to the re-birth of repressed nationalistic movements which ultimately led to the dissolution of Yugoslavia in 1991 and onwards. Croatia declared its independence in June 1991, which was accompanied by a war for independence that lasted until 1995. Croatia was widely recognized as an independent state in February 1992. Later that year Croatia became a part of the United Nations.

[08] In parallel with the dissolution of Yugoslavia and the war years, Croatia's economy went through a process of privatization. Privatization was until today seen as controversial and non-transparent, with a substantial portion of the country's wealth seen to be accumulated by politically well-connected individuals, leading some to characterise the Croatian economy of the 1990s as crony capitalism. Until 2000, Croatia was a semi-presidential republic under the heavy influence of then-president Franjo Tuđman. Constitutional changes in the early noughties transformed it to a parliamentary system of government, with a significant reduction in presidential powers. In 2013, Croatia became a European Union (EU) Member State, and as of 1 January 2023 it joined the Schengen Area and the Euro zone.

1.3 Legal System

[09] The Croatian legal system is based on the civil law system, in particular, the Germanic branch of civil law. The legal system is based on written sources of law, namely acts (adopted by the Parliament), delegated legislation (adopted by government or ministries), ratified international treaties, and EU law.

[10] Business people and legal practitioners often find the Croatian legal system over-bureaucratic and too formal. Over the last decade, the governments have systematically tried to reduce that burden, but this is often met with resistance from within the system and among the stakeholders, as well as by an inherent mentality that makes this a difficult task.

[11] Croatia ranked fifty-one out of 190 countries in the World Bank Ease of Doing Business Economy Rankings in 2020.

[12] Croatian legislation, with some exceptions such as the Maritime Code, is not codified but rather consists of different statutes. Business associations are regulated by the Companies Act, which is based predominantly on German (for stock corporations) and Austrian (for limited liability companies) laws. The Obligations Act was introduced in 2005 as an update of the Yugoslav Obligations Act from 1978, which was modelled most closely on Swiss obligations law. Land is characterised by double registration. Land ownership and other rights *in rem* are registered in the land registers organized as a separate division of the civil courts. In addition, the cadastre register keeps records of land plots and buildings erected on such land, as well as specific legal regimes on such plots. Cadastre also records possession over such land plots. As plots registered in the land register and the cadastre may be different, and since possessor and owner need not necessarily be the same person, sometimes the records from the land register and from the cadastre do not match. Since 2003, the Government has initiated a national program for aligning land registers and cadastres.

1.4 Cultural Aspects

[13] In general, Croatia is open to foreign investment. The Croatian legal environment is rather liberal as regards who can open and run a business in Croatia.

[14] Croatia is not an expensive place to do business, but there are regional differences: Zagreb and touristic areas are significantly more expensive places to do business than other regions where the costs of workforce and premises are lower

[15] While there are no local business practices or cultural issues which should represent a hurdle to a foreign investor, businessmen often find lawyers of government (central as well as local) to be difficult to handle. Many are sometimes prone to being stirred by NGOs and political parties in a direction that tends to favour the *status quo* and against investments that might change the local landscape. Lengthy court and other proceedings (whose outcome is frequently difficult to predict) are also seen by some as problematic.

2 THE REGULATORY FRAMEWORK

2.1 Companies Act

[16] The Companies Act (OG 111/93-18/23, hereinafter: the 'Companies Act') in the general form in which it is known today was passed in 1993 and came into force in 1995. The Act has been changed throughout the years, but the majority of changes have been passed in order to regulate certain situations, as well as rights and obligations, in more detail and to fill in gaps that have appeared in practice.

[17] One of the biggest changes has been allowing joint-stock companies to have a single-tier board instead of a two-tier board, which was usual in Croatia before 2007.

[18] The Companies Act does not systematically state which of its provisions are mandatory. Consequently, in some cases it is unclear whether a particular provision of the Companies Act is mandatory or whether companies are able to regulate a specific issue in a different way.

[19] Foreign companies and foreign sole proprietors are treated in the same way as domestic persons with respect to the conduct of business in the territory of the Republic of Croatia. However, unless a foreign investor incorporates a subsidiary, foreign companies and foreign sole proprietors may not permanently conduct business in the territory of the Republic of Croatia unless they establish a branch there. Occasional or one-time performance of an activity or of a particular work (the concept of the freedom to provide services in accordance with the EU acquis) is allowed without a branch or subsidiary.

2.2 Available Corporate Structures

[20] The following main corporate forms of entity are available in Croatia: limited liability company (*društvo s ograničenom odgovornošću or d.o.o.*), simple limited liability company (*jednostavno društvo s ograničenom odgovornošću or j.d.o.o.*), joint-stock company (*dioničko društvo or d.d.*), limited partnership (*komanditno društvo or k.d.*), economic interest grouping (*gospodarstvo interesno udruženje or GIU*), and general partnership (*javno trgovačko društvo or j.t.d.*).

[21] Additionally, individuals can register their 'sole proprietorship' (*obrt*) and carry out business activities as private entrepreneurs and sole traders.

[22] Foreign entities can establish any of these forms in Croatia but can also establish a branch office through which to carry out business activities in Croatia. Additionally, European Economic Interest Groupings and European Companies (Societas Europea) are also allowed to operate in Croatia.

2.3 Commercial Register

[23] All companies are legal entities and must be registered in the Commercial Register kept by the regional Commercial Courts of the region in which the company has its registered seat (the 'Commercial Register').

[24] In order for the company to be incorporated, it has to be registered with the Commercial Register of the relevant commercial court. The relevant commercial court will be determined by the seat of the company. The Commercial Register holds information on all limited liability companies and all joint-stock companies. All changes within the company must be duly reported and registered before the Commercial Register.

[25] Information and data contained in the Commercial Register are public and are presumed to be true and complete, meaning that a third party may rely on the information available in the Commercial Register. The Commercial Register is accessible over the Internet on https://sudreg.pravosudje.hr/registar/f?p=150:1. An official extract for the company can be obtained through the web page of the Commercial Register, directly at the Commercial Register or from a notary public.

[26] The Commercial Register is obligated to store a collection of documents regarding each company in hard copy. Such documents are articles of association/founding deeds, list of shareholders, certain resolutions of the general assembly etc. All documents deposited with the Commercial Register are accessible to the public. All documents must be submitted either in Croatian or with a verified translation to Croatian.

2.4 Data Mailboxes

[27] The Republic of Croatia has introduced a system for official electronic delivery of documents from public authorities to legal entities.

[28] A data mailbox is an electronic storage space similar to an email account which has been set up and is operated by the state. All companies have an obligation to register an email address with the Commercial Register for the purposes of electronic communication.

[29] The system of electronic delivery is still not entirely implemented and public authorities still deliver documents physically to the registered seat of the company more often than electronically.

2.5 Common Transactions

[30] Limited liability companies and joint-stock companies are the primary forms of companies involved in corporate mergers and acquisitions. Both are equity-based and have a registered capital contributed by their shareholder(s). They are both distinct legal entities and the financial liability of their shareholders is limited.

[31] Generally, both individuals and legal entities may enter into joint venture agreements, become a partner in a general commercial partnership, limited partnership, or silent partnership, or become a shareholder in a limited liability or joint-stock company. As far as sole ownership is concerned, generally, both a limited liability company and a joint-stock company may have a sole owner, and both may be the sole owner of another company. Thus, for example, a limited liability company may become the sole shareholder of a joint-stock company or vice versa. Other types of entrepreneurial entities may also become the sole owner of a joint-stock company or a limited liability company. Furthermore, two or more companies may be merged or consolidated into one company without liquidation of the companies.

2.6 Comparison of Limited Liability Company and Joint-Stock Company

[32] Most common type of company in Croatia is a limited liability company, as well as joint-stock company.

	Limited Liability Company	*Joint-Stock Company*
Basic characteristics	Limited liability company (*društvo s ograničenom odgovornošću* or *d.o.o.*) is a type of company generally preferred by investors with a limited number of investors who plan to hold their investments in the company for the mid- to long-term. A limited liability company is typically used by small- to medium-sized enterprises.	Joint-stock Company (*dioničko društvo* or *d.d.*) is a type of company generally preferred by large enterprises and enterprises who want to be listed on the stock exchange.
Incorporation	Limited liability company (LLC) may be incorporated by one or more shareholders (without limit). Shareholders may be natural or legal persons. Shareholder of an LLC cannot be a person: Convicted for the criminal offence of terrorist financing or the criminal offence of money laundering while the legal consequences of the conviction are in force; in respect of whom international measures limiting the disposal of assets have been introduced, while these measures are in force. In case of a sole shareholder, the founding deed will be statement of incorporation and in case of more shareholders, the founding deed will be articles of association, but both need to be issued in the form of a notarial deed. Company is incorporated once it is registered before the Commercial Register. Shareholders of the limited liability company are registered and visible in the Commercial Register.	Joint-stock company may be incorporated by one or more founders (without limit). Founders may be natural or legal persons. Prohibitions for being a shareholder of a joint-stock company are the same as for the limited liability company – see the left column. Founding deed of a joint-stock company is the articles of association (statute). The statute must be issued in a form of notarial deed. Company is incorporated once it is registered before the Commercial Register. Shareholders of the joint-stock company are not visible in the Commercial Register. However, if a joint-stock company has only one shareholder, it must be registered in the Commercial Register. Shareholders in a joint-stock company are registered with the Central Depositary and Clearing Company.

	Limited Liability Company	*Joint-Stock Company*
Share capital	Share capital of an LLC is paid by the shareholders, in accordance with their business shares. As of 1 January 2023, when the euro became the official currency in Croatia, the minimum share capital is EUR2 500 00. Share capital expressed in HRK will have to be expressed in EUR amount. Nominal amount of one business share cannot be less than EUR1 000.	Share capital of the joint-stock company is paid by the shareholders, in accordance with their shares. As of January 2023 the minimum share capital is EUR2 500 000. Share capital expressed in HRK will have to be expressed in EUR amount. As of 1 January 2023 minimum nominal amount of one share is EUR100). It is also possible to issue shares without a nominal value. In that case, share in the share capital is determined by the total number of shares.
	Contributions to the share capital of a limited liability company can be financial or in-kind.	Contributions to the share capital of a joint-stock company can be financial or in-kind.
	Prior to incorporation, share capital can be paid in full or at least as to 25% with obligation that full amount of share capital is paid within one year of incorporation. Each shareholder must pay at least 25% of his contribution prior to incorporation.	Prior to incorporation, share capital can be paid in full or at least as to 25%.
	Non-monetary contributions must be made in full before the registration before the Commercial Register.	Non-monetary contributions must be made in full before the registration before the Commercial Register.
	Articles of association can stipulate that shareholders have an obligation to make additional contributions outside the registered capital of the company. Companies Act regulates that such decision can be made unanimously by all shareholders of the limited liability company, but the articles of association can also regulate that such decision is made by a three-quarters majority of shareholders. The size of such mandatory contributions is not limited by the Companies Act. The shareholders can stipulate such limitations in the articles of association.	Statute of a joint-stock company can stipulate that shareholders have an obligation to make additional contributions outside the share capital of the company. The size of such mandatory contributions is not limited by the Companies Act. The shareholders can stipulate such limitations in the articles of association.

	Limited Liability Company	*Joint-Stock Company*
	To protect shareholders against unreasonable mandatory contributions, the Companies Act introduces the right of any shareholder who did not agree to the mandatory contribution to exit the company.	
Ownership interest	Limited liability company does not issue shares.	
Shares	The ownership interest represents the shareholder's participation in the company and the rights and duties derive from participation. The size of ownership interest is determined by the ratio of a shareholder's investment contribution to the company's share capital (unless the articles of association regulate otherwise).	A joint-stock company may have: – registered shares (issued to a named shareholder) in physical or electronic form; – bearer shares in physical form. In 2008, it was prohibited for any joint-stock company to issue bearer shares. However, previously issued bearer shares were not rescinded. A joint-stock company may issue common shares and priority shares. Common shares entitle their holder to: – the right to vote in the General Meeting of the company; – the right to be paid part of the company's profit; – the right to be paid a part of the remaining liquidation or insolvency assets of the company. Priority shares entitle their holder to certain privileged rights, such as priority during payment of part of company's profit, right to be paid part of company's profit in a predetermined amount etc. Priority shares can be issued without the voting rights for their holders.
	Ownership of shares in a limited liability company can be transferred to another person by a written and notarized transfer agreement. Depending on the powers of other shareholders, as regulated by the articles of association, an approval of the general meeting may or may not be required for transfer of shares. For the completion of transfer of shares, the transfer must be registered in the Commercial Register	Shares in electronic form are transferred by crediting them to the account of the acquirer held by Central Depository and Clearing Company. Ownership of bearer shares may be transferred by simple handover of the document. Paper shares can also be transferred by endorsement, a special statement by which the shareholder transfers the share to another person. Articles of association may require consent of the company (given by the

	Limited Liability Company	*Joint-Stock Company*
	and must be noted in the share ledger of the limited liability company.	management board) for transfer of paper shares.
Articles of Association limited liability company) **or** **Statute (joint-stock company)**	Articles of association must be prepared in the form of notarial deed. Companies Act regulates structure and obligations related to the limited liability company liberally. Articles of Association may deviate from the provision of the Companies Act in all cases in which the Companies Act do not prohibit deviation.	Statute must be adopted in the form of notarial deed. Companies Act regulates structure and obligations of joint-stock companies more strictly than limited liability companies. Articles of Association may deviate from the provision of the Companies Act only in cases in which Companies Act allow deviation.
Corporate bodies	Corporate governance of a limited liability company is simpler than corporate governance of a joint-stock company.	The corporate governance of a joint-stock company is more complex than that of a limited liability company.
Corporate bodies	**Corporate Structure** An LLC is obligated to have: – general meeting; – management board Supervisory board is obligatory in certain cases, but an LLC may appoint a supervisory board even if it is not mandatory.	**Corporate Structure** There are two possible structure for joint-stock company: (i) dualistic structure (with management board and supervisory board) (ii) monistic structure (with board of directors) Statute of joint-stock company must state the corporate structure of the joint-stock company. **Dualistic structure** In a dualistic system, bodies of the joint-stock company are: – General Assembly, – Management Board, – Supervisory Board
Management Board	**Acting on behalf of a company** Unless the articles of association regulate otherwise, all members of the management board can represent the company and take actions in the name of the company jointly.	**Acting on behalf of a company** Unless the statute state otherwise, members of the board of directors represent the company jointly and may jointly perform acts of law that are binding on the joint-stock company.

	Limited Liability Company	*Joint-Stock Company*
	If articles of association authorize members of the management board to represent the company and take actions in the name of the company solely and independently, a member is not allowed to take any action if another member objects to taking such action. Articles can also regulate that certain members may take actions regardless of the objection of other members of the management board. Information whether a member of the management board may act solely and independently or jointly must be registered in the Commercial Register. Authority to represent may be further limited for individual member, but such limitations do not have any effect to third parties. Decisions of the members of the executive body on the business management of a company are taken by a simple majority of votes, unless regulated otherwise by the articles of association.	Information on whether a member of the board of directors may act independently or whether the articles of association require members of the board of directors to act jointly must be registered in the Commercial Register. Decisions of the board of directors are taken by a simple majority or another majority specified in the articles of association. In case of a tie in votes, a decision will be made by the chairman of the board, unless otherwise specified in the statute.
	Members of the Management Board General Meeting appoints and revokes the members of the Management Board, unless Articles of Association state otherwise. Minimum number of board members is one. Member of the Management Board cannot be a person: – Convicted for the criminal offence of money laundering, terrorist financing, abuse of trust in business operations, fraud in business operations, causing bankruptcy, favouring creditors or violating the obligation to keep trade and business	**Members of the Management Board** Supervisory Board appoints and recalls members of the Management Board. Members of the Management Board may be appointed for a term of up to five years. Members may be re-appointed. Minimum number of board members is one. If the management board consists of more than one person, a chairman of the management board must be appointed. Prohibitions for appointment of members of Management Board are the same as for the limited liability company – see the left column.

Limited Liability Company	Joint-Stock Company
books from the Criminal Code of the Republic of Croatia or previously valid criminal offenses of bankruptcy abuse and abuse in bankruptcy proceedings, and for the time that the legal consequences of the conviction last, as well as for which an international measure to limit the disposal of assets has been introduced, while such a measure is in force; – convicted of a criminal offense of another state which, according to its essential characteristics, corresponds to the criminal offenses from the previous point; – against whom a security measure of prohibition to perform an occupation, which is fully or partially covered by the subject of the company's business for the duration of that prohibition, has been imposed; – who is prohibited in another state from practicing an occupation that is fully or partially covered by the subject of the company's business for the duration of the prohibition	
Duty of care Members of the management board must manage business affairs of the company with the care of a diligent manager and keep business secret. Members of the management board that breach their obligations, are responsible for damages as joint debtors. In case of a dispute, they must prove that they have applied the care of a diligent manager.	**Duty of care** Members of company bodies must act with the care of a diligent manager and their responsibility cannot be limited or excluded. The rules applicable to members of company bodies in a limited liability company relating to the duty of care, business judgment, receiving orders from other corporate bodies, the legal relationship of the members of the company bodies with the company, and consequences of a breach of their duties also

	Limited Liability Company	*Joint-Stock Company*
	Member(s) of the Management Board will not be liable for damages if they have been conducting business in accordance with the decision of the General Meeting. Member(s) of the Management Board will not be liable for damages, even if their decision causes loss for a company, if they had acted on the basis of sufficient information in the justifiable interests of (and with loyalty to) a company. A breach of the duty to act with the care of a diligent business person may result in the executive director: – being obliged to pay damages (either to the company or to the shareholders); – being criminally liable for breach of his duties; – being prohibited by a court from performing activities of an executive director for a period of up to ten years or indefinitely.	apply to members of the bodies of a joint-stock company – See the left column.
Supervisory Board	Supervisory board is obligatory in the following cases: – if average annual number of employees is over 200; – if share capital of the company is higher than EUR80.00 000 and the company has more than 50 shareholders; – if the company performs certain business activity for which supervisory board is mandatory; – if the LLC solely manages joint-stock companies or limited liability companies obligated to have a supervisory board; or participates in them with more than 50% in direct share in the	A joint-stock company with a dualistic management structure must have a supervisory board, which is obliged to oversee the manner in which the board of directors exercises its powers and the manner in which the business of the joint-stock company is conducted. For this purpose, it has the right to examine all the records and documents of the joint-stock company (including the financial statements and minutes of the board of directors), to convene a general meeting of shareholders under certain circumstances, and to represent the joint-stock company in actions against members of the board of directors. The members of a supervisory board must act with the care of a diligent manager.

Limited Liability Company	*Joint-Stock Company*
share capital, and in both cases the average number of employees in one company or all companies together is over 200; – if the LLC is a general partner in a limited partnership and the average number of employees in the limited partnership together is over 200.	The supervisory board reviews the annual, extraordinary and consolidated financial accounts, and, if applicable, interim financial accounts and proposals for profit distribution and coverage of losses, and submits its comments to the general meeting. Interim financial accounts and proposals for profit distribution and coverage of losses and submits its comments to the general meeting. The supervisory board is entitled to convene a general meeting, if the interests of the company so require. Supervisory board represents the company before the Management Board.
Members of the Supervisory Board Minimum number of members of the Supervisory Board is three. There must always be an odd number of members. General Meeting appoints and revokes members of the Supervisory Board. Members of the Supervisory Board chose the Chairman and Vice-Chairman between them. Term of a member of a management board is four years and they may be appointed again. Member of a Supervisory Board cannot be a person that does not fulfil conditions to be appointed as a member of a Management Board.	Minimum number of members of the supervisory board is three. Number of members may be higher, but in any case, it must be an odd number. Maximum number of members of the supervisory board depends on the share capital of the company: – up to EUR1.50 000 – max. nine members; – between EUR1.500.00 000 and EUR10.000.00 000 – max. fifteen members; – over EUR10.000.00 000– max. twenty-one members. Members of the Supervisory Board are appointed by the General Meeting of the company, unless otherwise regulated by the Statute of the company. Supervisory Board members may be appointed for a maximum term of four years, but they may be re-appointed. **Monistic structure** In a monistic system, bodies of the joint-stock company are: – General Assembly, – Board of Directors

	Limited Liability Company	*Joint-Stock Company*
Board of directors		The board of directors organizes the company internally, monitors performing of company's affairs, appoints executive directors, represents the company before executive directors etc. Executive directors represent the company. Unless the statute states otherwise, executive directors represent the company jointly. Alternatively, instead of a board of directors and a supervisory board, a joint-stock company may have an board of directors. Minimum number of members of the Board of directors is three. Members may be appointed for a term up to six years and may be re-appointed. Board of directors elects executive directors for a period up to six years. Executive director does not have to be a member of the Board of directors. Executive directors represent and manage business affairs of the company.
Shareholder's Rights	General Meeting consists of all shareholders of the limited liability company. The rights of shareholders in a limited liability company are broadly similar to the rights of shareholders in a joint-stock company – see the right column.	General Meeting consists of all shareholders of the joint-stock company. Shareholders are entitled at the general meeting to inspect and approve the financial statements of a joint-stock company and the reports prepared by the board of directors and the supervisory board. At the general meeting, shareholders may appoint and recall the members of the Supervisory Board. No shareholder is entitled to receive any business-related information from the management of a company other than the reports and other information provided to all shareholders. Shareholders participate in the profits of the joint-stock company through dividends approved by the General Assembly of shareholders. Dividends may only be paid when the General Assembly has approved the payment of dividends on the basis of the company's economic

Limited Liability Company	*Joint-Stock Company*
	performance, as set out in the annual financial statement. Companies Act allows the making of dividend prepayments (interim dividends) before the general meeting has decided to pay dividends. The interim dividends may be paid out only on the basis of interim financial statements which will confirm that the company has enough funds to distribute profit and in compliance with further rules stipulated by the Companies Act as to which company funds may be used and to what extent. Dividends or interim dividends may not be paid out if it would render the company insolvent. Dividends or interim dividends can be paid out to the shareholders only after: – any losses from previous years have been settled; – regulated amounts have been paid to the legal reserves; – regulated amounts have been paid to the reserves for the own shares of the company (if the company intends to acquire them); – regulated amounts have been paid to the statutory reserves. Minority shareholders holding shares whose total nominal value or number of shares amounts to 5% of the share capital may request that the board of directors convene a general meeting with an agenda proposed by the minority shareholders. Each shareholder is also generally entitled to challenge a decision of the general meeting in court. All shareholders have a pre-emptive right under the Companies Act to subscribe to newly issued shares (if the shares are to be subscribed for monetary consideration – i.e., not in the case of in-kind consideration). The pre-emptive right may be limited or excluded by a decision of the general meeting made by three-fourth majority of shareholders.

	Limited Liability Company	*Joint-Stock Company*
Controlling relationship	See the right column which also applies to limited liability companies.	Companies Act distinguishes three levels of control under Croatian law: (i) majority share; (ii) control; and (iii) concern, and sets out the legal regime governing them. Majority share – an entity that has majority share or majority decision-making rights in another company. Controlling entity – a controlling entity is an entity which may directly or indirectly exercise decisive influence over the company. It is considered that an entity has a controlling position over a company if it has the right to appoint and revoke majority of the Management Board, Supervisory Board or Board of directors members Concern – one influential or controlling entity and one or more dependant entities are subjected to uniform control of the influential or controlling entity. All companies together form a concern and each company independently is a concern company.

2.7 Ultimate Beneficial Owners Registry

[33] The Anti-money Laundering and Financing of Terrorism Act (Official Gazette 108/18-151/22, hereinafter the 'UBO Act') regulates obligations for companies to register their ultimate beneficial owner to the Ultimate Beneficial Owners Registry managed by the Croatian Financial Agency.

[34] Once a company is incorporated, it has to submit an application for registration of its ultimate beneficial owner of the company to the Ultimate Beneficial Owners Registry. The same procedure applies when a shareholder of a company changes. The deadline for submitting the application is thirty days from registration of incorporation or change of ownership before the Commercial Register. In accordance with Croatian legislation, the ultimate beneficial owner is any natural person who owns at least 25% in the equity of the legal entity or a natural person who has prevailing influence on the business activities of the legal entity. In case the beneficial owner of the legal entity cannot be determined by this criteria, the authorized representative(s) of the legal entity have to be registered as the beneficial owner(s).

[35] Key information in the Ultimate Beneficial Owners Registry is publicly available via online government system e-građani. It is to be expected that the public availability of such data may be limited in the future in accordance with a European Court judgment in joined cases C-37/20 Luxembourg Business Registers and C-601/20 Sovim, which ruled that accessibility in all cases to any member of the general public information on UBOs was illegal.

[36] If the company does not comply with its obligations under the UBO Act, a company may face a monetary fine in the amount of EUR66 000–46.450 00) and the responsible individual of the legal person may face a monetary fine in the amount of EUR66 000–9.95 000).

3 LAWS AFFECTING M&A

3.1 Regulatory Framework

[37] In addition to the Companies Act, mergers and acquisition of companies in Croatia will be affected by the following laws:

- Companies Act (OG 111/93-18/23).
- Act on Ownership And Other Rights In Rem (OG 91/96-152/14).
- Civil Obligations Act (OG 35/05-156/22).
- Capital Markets Act (OG 65/18-151/22).
- Takeover of Joint-Stock Companies Act (OG 109/07-148/13).
- Commercial Register Act (OG 1/95-34/22).
- Competition Act (OG 79/09-41/21).
- General Tax Act (OG 115/16-114/22).
- Insolvency Act (OG 71/15-36/22).
- Act on Private International Law (OG 101/17).
- The UBO Act.
- Criminal Code (OG 125/11-114/22).
- Criminal Procedure Act (OG 152/08-80/22).
- Act on Criminal Liability of Legal Entities (OG 151/03-114/22).
- Act on Introduction of European Company – Societas Europea (SE) and European Cooperative Society (EGIU) (OG 107/07-11/15).

[38] Various sectoral laws, including:

- Credit Institutions Act (OG 159/13, 19/15, 102/15, 15/18, 70/19, 47/20, 146/20, 151/22).
- Insurance Act (OG 30/15-151/22).
- Act on Open Investment Funds with Public Offering (OG 44/16-76/22).
- Act on Alternative Investment Funds (OG 21/18-110/21).
- Media Act (OG 59/04, 84/11, 81/13, 114/22).
- Electronic Communications Act (NN 76/22).
- Electronic Media Act (OG 111/21, 114/22).

4 TRANSFORMATIONS

4.1 General Framework

[39] Croatian law provides a variety of possibilities in terms of transformations of the company, but the general rule is that there are no transformations other than those prescribed under the law. It is possible to transform a company's legal form, e.g., transforming a joint-stock company into a limited liability company (or the other way around) or a joint-stock company to a general partnership. In addition to transforming companies, Croatian law also allows mergers and demergers of companies and cross-border mergers and demergers. In addition, combining more types of transformations at once – for example a merger involving transformation of the legal form (transforming a joint-stock company into a limited liability company and merging to another limited liability company) – is also allowed. In each case of transformation, where the company ceases to exist after the transformation, liquidation of the dissolving company is not required.

[40] A transformation can be prohibited under the Act on Liability of Legal Persons for Criminal Acts if the transformation would lead to the cessation of the company which is charged with a criminal offence.

[41] The legal framework for transformations is the Companies Act (which incorporates the European legislation in that respect).

[42] The following types of transformation are possible under Croatian law:

- Merger by acquisition [*pripajanje društava*]
- Merger by consolidation [*spajanje društava*]
- Cross-border mergers and demergers
- Demerger of the company [*podjela društva*]
- Transformation of the company's legal form.

4.2 Mergers

4.2.1 Merger by Acquisition

[43] In the event of a merger by acquisition, one or more companies are dissolved by transferring their entire business assets (merged companies) to another company (acquiring company). The principle is that shareholders of merged companies become shareholders of the acquiring company.

4.2.2 Merger by Consolidation

[44] In the event of a merger by consolidation, two or more companies are dissolved, and their business assets are transferred to a newly established company. Merger by consolidation is possible under Croatian law only if each company is duly registered in the court registry for at least two years prior to the resolution on merger by consolidation.

4.3 Cross-Border Transformations

[45] The Companies Act allows the majority of domestic transformations to be carried out on a cross-border basis. The Croatian legislation is entirely in line with the EU legislation (EU Directive 2005/56/EC).

4.4 Demerger

[46] There are two types of demergers under Croatian law:

(i) Demerger by splitting (where the demerged entity ceases to exist) including:
   (a) Demerger by splitting where the property (assets and liabilities) of the demerged company are transferred to newly established company or companies.
   (b) Demerger by splitting where the property (assets and liabilities) of the demerged company is transferred to already existing successor companies.
   (c) A combination of methods under (a) and (b).

[47] In this case, the liquidation of the company is not required:

(ii) Demerger by spin-off (where the demerged entity survives the demerger) including:
   (a) Demerger by spin-off where part of the company (assets and liabilities) of the emerged company is transferred to a newly established company or companies.
   (b) Demerger by spin-off where part of the company (assets and liabilities) of the emerged company is transferred to an already existing successor company or companies.
   (c) A combination of methods under (a) and (b) paragraph **[43]**. While the division plan allocates assets and liabilities between demerged companies, all companies that took part in the demerger remain liable for obligations of the demerged company that arose before the demerger was registered in the commercial court register.

4.5 Transformation of a Legal Form

[48] Croatian law provides a variety of possibilities in terms of the transformation of companies. It is important to emphasize that the transformation of legal form does not change the identity of the legal entity. The basic rule is that there is no legal succession after the transformation is finalized, but the shareholders are protected by the principle of continuity.

[49] Transformation of legal form of a company requires a registration in the court registry. The procedure of transformation, as well as the permitted legal form to which a company might be transformed depends on the type of company being transformed.

5 RELEVANT REGULATORY AUTHORITIES

[50] The competent national regulatory authority for merger control is the Agency for the Protection of Competition (the 'Agency'). The Agency's job is to make sure that different kinds of anticompetitive practices are detected, assessed and sanctioned if they represent infringements of competition rules. It is responsible for the implementation of the Croatian Competition Act. The same applies to the assessment of compatibility of concentrations (mergers and acquisitions). The EU competition rules are also directly applicable.

[51] Although general authority for merger control lies within the scope of the Agency's competence, there are several derogations depending on a specific sector. Below is a list of several of the most significant regulatory authorities.

[52] The Croatian National Bank in specific cases is required to grant an authorization for acquiring certain shareholdings in a credit institution pursuant to the Croatian Credit Institutions Act.

[53] The Croatian Financial Services Supervisory Agency (HANFA) is the regulator of non-banking financial activities. An entity acquiring a holding in a leasing, factoring, insurance or reinsurance, pension insurance, investment company, stock exchange, fund management company may need, depending on the type of the target and on the acquiring shareholding, prior authorization from HANFA. HANFA also supervises certain other matters related to transformation of companies. It is also competent for matters related to public takeover bids.

[54] The Croatian Regulatory Authority for Network Industries supervises electronic communications operators. All electronic communications operators with significant market power, or those with license to use the radio frequency spectrum are required to inform the Croatian Regulatory Authority for Network Industries on any merger.

[55] Each of these regulatory authorities is governed by different laws and some are more and others less flexible when it comes to timing, information sharing and granting required approvals. In addition, sectoral laws in other industries regulate different aspects that may have impact on mergers and acquisitions of entities operating in these fields.

6 CONTROLS/RESTRICTIONS ON FOREIGN INVESTMENT

[56] As of 3 October 2020, the Regulation on the implementation of the EU FDI Regulation (Regulation (EU) 2019/452) of The European Parliament and of the Council of 19 March 2019 is in force. The FDI Regulation has established the National Contact Point and the Interdepartmental Commission which both act as a competent authority for the implementation of the EU FDI Regulation. In practice, the National Contact Point will have the power to request information from the foreign investor intending to invest in Croatia or an undertaking located in Croatia in which the direct foreign investment is planned to be realized or has already been realized.

6.1 Acquisition of Real Estate by Foreigners

[57] Although the EU prohibits restrictions on the acquisition of real estate in its Member States, before joining the EU, Croatia agreed on a transitional period during which it could impose restrictions on the acquisition of agricultural land.

[58] The first transitional period was seven years from Croatia joining the EU. This initial period was prolonged for an additional three-year period and it will expire on 23 June 2023. Once expired, there will be no restrictions and all foreigners will be able to acquire agricultural land.

7 ACQUISITION OF REGULATED ENTITIES

[59] The acquisition by an entity or entities acting in concert of a 'qualified shareholding' or shares above certain thresholds in a regulated entity is conditional upon obtaining prior approval from the relevant regulatory authority. A qualified shareholding means a direct or indirect shareholding which (a) represents 10% or more of the capital or voting rights; or (b) enables the exercise of significant influence over the management of the acquired entity.

[60] Failure to obtain approval does not invalidate the sale, but usually leads to some form of suspension of voting rights.

7.1 Banks

[61] Under the Credit Institutions Act, the direct or indirect acquisition by an entity or entities acting in concert of a qualified shareholding (as defined in paragraph **[67]**) in a bank[1] is subject to the prior approval of the Croatian National

[1] Or other credit institution – savings bank, house savings bank and credit institution from Art. 4/1/1/b of the EU Regulation 575/2013.

Bank (CNB). The same applies if an entity or entities acting in concert intends to increase their direct or indirect shareholding to (or above) 20%, 30% or 50% of the voting rights or share capital of the bank.

[62] A share acquisition made without the prior approval of the CNB remains valid. However, in such cases the voting rights attached to the shares exceeding the applicable threshold cannot be exercised and the acquiring entity or entities acting in concert must sell the respective shares within the deadline that CNB determines in its decision.

[63] If an entity decides to transfer or otherwise reduce its qualified shareholding in a credit institution below the applicable threshold, it must notify the CNB of such decision.

[64] Failure to comply with the above obligations may result in misdemeanour sanctions.

7.2 Investment Firms

[65] Under the Capital Markets Act, the direct or indirect acquisition by an entity or entities acting in concert of a qualified shareholding in an investment firm is subject to the prior approval of the Croatian Financial Services Supervisory Agency (HANFA). The same applies if an entity or entities acting in concert intend to increase their direct or indirect shareholding resulting in the acquisition of 10%, 20%, 30% or 50% of the voting rights or share capital of the investment firm or in gaining control over the investment firm.

[66] A share acquisition made without the prior approval of the HANFA is valid. However, in such case voting rights attached to the shares exceeding the applicable threshold cannot be exercised and the acquiring entity or entities acting in concert must sell the respective shares within the deadline the HANFA determines in its decision.

[67] If an entity decides to transfer its qualified shareholding in an investment firm, or if its qualified shareholding reduces so that it amounts to or is smaller than the applicable thresholds, or so that such entity ceases to be the controlling entity of the investment firm, it must notify the HANFA of such transaction.

[68] Failure to comply with the above obligations may result in misdemeanour sanctions.

7.3 Central Securities Depository and Organizers of Regulated Markets

[69] Under the Capital Markets Act, the direct or indirect acquisition by an entity or entities acting in concert of a qualified shareholding in a central securities depository resulting in the acquisition of 20%, 30% or 50% of the voting rights or share capital of the central securities depository or in gaining control over the central securities depository, is subject to the prior approval of the HANFA.

7.4 Management Companies and Investment Funds

[70] Rules applicable to the acquisition of qualified shareholding in UCITS fund management companies are to a great extent similar to those applicable to investment firms[2]. The act regulating this matter is the Investment Funds with Public Offer Act.

[71] With regard to alternative investment funds (AIF) management companies, the Alternative Investment Funds Act applies and differentiates the procedures with regard to large investment funds and medium and small investment funds.

[72] With regard to large alternative investment funds, rules applicable to acquisition of qualified shareholding are materially the same as those that apply to the acquisition of qualified shareholdings in UCITS fund management companies.

[73] With regard to medium and small alternative investment funds, the direct or indirect acquisition by an entity or entities acting in concert of a qualified shareholding in management company resulting in the acquisition of 10%, 20%, 30% or 50% of the voting rights or share capital, or in gaining control over the management company, must be notified to the management company itself. The management company then has to notify HANFA which must within thirty days decide on potential restrictions. If no decision within the deadline is rendered, the acquisition can be implemented.

[74] If an entity decides to transfer its qualified shareholding in a medium and small AIF management company, or if its qualified shareholding reduces so that it amounts to or is smaller than the applicable thresholds, or so that such entity ceases to be the controlling entity, it must notify the HANFA of such transaction.

[75] Failure to comply with the above obligations may result in misdemeanour sanctions.

7.5 Pension Companies Managing Obligatory Pension Funds

[76] Under the Obligatory Pension Funds Act, any change in shareholding of the pension company managing obligatory pension funds ('Obligatory Pension Company') is subject to HANFA's prior approval.

[77] A share disposition made without the prior approval of the HANFA is null and void.

[2] One material difference is non appliance of the 10% threshold.

[78] The same legal or natural person can be a shareholder only in one Obligatory Pension Company. In case of any subsequent acquisition of shares in another Obligatory Pension Company, voting rights or other management rights attached to the subsequently acquired shares cannot be exercised.

7.6 Pension Companies Managing Voluntary Pension Funds

[79] Acquisition and disposal of shares in pension companies managing voluntary pension funds is regulated by the Voluntary Pension Funds Act.

[80] Acquisition of qualified shareholding is subject to similar rules and procedures as with respect to investment firms described above (7.2. Investment Firms section).

7.7 Insurance/Reinsurance Companies

[81] Acquisition and disposal of shares in insurance/reinsurance companies is regulated by the Insurance Act.

[82] Acquisition of qualified shareholding is subject to similar rules and procedures as with respect to investment firms described above (section 7.2. Investment Firms).

7.8 Credit Unions

[83] There is no regulatory approval process for becoming a member of a credit union according to the Credit Unions Act. The decision on access to or withdrawal from the union's membership lies with the credit union itself, not the regulator.

7.9 Payment Institutions

[84] Acquisitions and disposals of shares in payment institutions is regulated by the Payment System Act.

[85] Acquisitions of qualified shareholdings are subject to similar rules and procedures as with respect to credit institutions described above (section 7.1. Banks). The obligation to sell acquired shares is subject to the CNB's determination that there is no possibility of the acquirer having a negative influence on the management of the payment institution, in which case such sale need not be carried out.

7.10 Other Specific Industries

[86] Generally speaking – similar restrictions or other formalities exist with regard to other specific industries/activities such as factoring (Factoring Act regulating factoring companies), leasing (Leasing Act regulating leasing companies), exchange (Foreign Exchange Act regulating cash exchange companies), electronic money (Electronic Money Act regulating electronic money institutions), media (Media Act) or electronic media (Electronic Media Act).

8 INCENTIVES FOR FOREIGN INVESTMENT

8.1 General Information

[87] Investors who invest in Croatia can obtain aid in the form of investment incentives. The beneficiary of investment incentives may be any entrepreneur (legal or natural person) whose business is registered in Croatia.

8.2 Current Forms of Investment Incentives

[88] Investment incentives exist in the following forms:

(1) tax subsidies;
(2) support for new jobs/training related to investment projects;
(3) grants for:
  - development and innovation activities;
  - business support activities;
  - high-added value service activities;
(4) support for capital costs of investment projects;
(5) support for labour-intensive investment projects;
(6) support for the economic activation of inactive assets owned by Croatia;
(7) support for the modernization of businesses – automation, robotization and digitization of production and processing processes.

8.3 Competent investment authority

[89] Investors apply for incentives to the Ministry of Economy and Sustainable Development. Upon receiving the application, the Ministry, together with other administrative authorities competent for the industry in question, determines whether the request is justified and informs the entrepreneur within sixty days.

[90] An investor who has been granted incentives must provide the Ministry with regular reports on the project which is supported by the incentives.

9 SPECIFIC ISSUES OF COMPANY/SECURITIES LAW

9.1 Financial Assistance

[91] A joint-stock company is not allowed to grant an advance payment, a loan or to provide a security for the purpose of acquiring shares in that joint-stock company (financial assistance). Legal transactions contrary to the financial assistance rules are null and void.

[92] The prohibition of financial assistance does not apply to:

- regular business credit/financial institutions, under certain further formalities;
- financial assistance for the acquisition of shares for employees in the JSC or employees in the affiliated JSC, under certain further formalities.

[93] In case of otherwise allowed financial assistance (i.e., cases described in the previous paragraph), when the purpose of such transaction is the acquisition of the JSC's own shares by members of the management or supervisory board, by the parent company or by third persons acting for the account of these entities, the transaction will be null and void unless it is in JSC's 'best interest'. The latter term is not explicitly defined and will be assessed on a case-by-case basis.

[94] The prohibition of financial assistance does not apply to non-JSC companies (limited liability companies, most notably).

9.2 Security Interests

[95] Types of security interest in Croatia are security interests over movable assets, over real estate (mortgages) and over receivables (and other individual rights which can be 'cashed out').

[96] Security is accessory in nature and there is no security without secured debt. There is an exception to this rule: an 'un-erased mortgage' – i.e., a security interest on real estate that exists even after the full settlement of the debt which it secured and which can be used to secure another debt of the debtor.

[97] A foreign lender may take security over local movable or immovable property as well as receivables.

[98] There is a concept of a 'floating pledge' which is generically defined and covers all assets owned or used by the security provider, which are situated in a certain, defined space (e.g., a warehouse, business premises). It is not recommended to rely solely on this type of pledge. The reason is that the individual assets under the floating pledge are freely transferable. Although the debtor should maintain the value of the assets under the floating pledge, it may happen that at the time of enforcement of the pledge, no valuable assets remain. In such scenario the secured creditor would have no proprietary rights against the individual persons that acquired the respective assets.

[99] There is no singular security register. Generally, the perfection of the security requires the entry of the security into specific registers:

- a mortgage needs to be entered into the Land Register kept by competent municipal courts;
- charges over movables or receivables must be signed as a notarial deed (or before a court) and registered with the Registry of Court and Notarial Securities which is kept by the Financial Agency (exceptions are security interests where the possession of collateral is transferred);
- security interests over vehicles, airplanes and ships need to be entered into specific registries or sub registries for these types of movable assets;
- security interests over securities are registered on the account of the secured creditor held with the Central Depository and Clearing Company;
- security interests over certain intellectual property rights (e.g., trademarks) can be registered in pertinent registers of intellectual property rights.

[100] Even in cases where the entry of the security into specific registers is not a prerequisite for the perfection of the security, registration with the competent register (if allowed) is always recommended as it makes the existence of the pledge public/apparent to all third persons.

[101] Some of the registers are publicly accessible while others can only be searched upon proving a legitimate interest in doing so. There is no all-purpose search of security provided by a party – searches depend on some information about collateral being available.

[102] Croatian versions of the security agreements (a signed Croatian version or an official translation into Croatian) need to be presented to the registration authority in order for the registration to proceed.

9.3 Completion Formalities

Asset	*Formalities*
Real estate	A written agreement with a notarized signature and the registration of the transfer of an ownership right in the Land Register is required for the transfer of real estate.
Share in limited liability company	A solemnized notarial written agreement is required for a transfer of a share in a limited liability company. The transfer has to be registered in the Commercial Register and in the share register maintained by the management of the company whose share is being transferred.

Asset	*Formalities*
Enterprise	There are no specific rules on the transfer of an enterprise, i.e., specific rules for transfer of particular assets that are encompassed by the enterprise should be followed. Nevertheless, it should be noted that a person to whom a whole or a part of an enterprise has been transferred shall be liable for debts in connection with the transferred enterprise, jointly with the previous transferor, but only up to the value of the transferred assets.
Movable Property	An agreement is required for the transfer of title to movable property to the purchaser. Generally, the transfer agreement as such does not need to be in writing, but a written form is recommended. This is not the case for specific types of movable property (e.g., vehicles, boats, planes) which require a written agreement.
Receivables	Receivables are transferred by an assignment agreement. Unless agreed otherwise between the parties in the contract giving rise to the receivable in question, the debtor's consent to the assignment is not required. Once the assignment is notified to the debtor by the assignor or proven by the assignee, the debtor can discharge its obligation only by performing its obligations to the assignee and not to the assignor.
Agreements	An agreement may be transferred with the consent of all the parties to the agreement. The consent must be in the same form as is prerequisite for the validity of the transferred agreement. The transferor is liable to the transferee for the validity of the transferred contract. Transferor's liability for due execution of obligations by the other party (to the transferee) or the transferee (to the other party) must be specifically stipulated.
Intellectual Property Rights	The transfer of industrial intellectual property rights must be registered in a public register. Copyrights as such cannot be transferred but individual underlying rights may be transferred.
Licences	Licences granted under public law may not generally be transferred.

Asset	*Formalities*
Employees	In case of transfer of an enterprise or a part thereof (which retains its economic integrity), the employment agreements of the affected workers are transferred by operation of law. Generally, employees retain all rights they acquired up to the date of the transfer. The new employer to which the enterprise or its part has been transferred will be liable for obligations towards the transferred employees jointly with the previous employer.

10 INSOLVENCY

10.1 General

[103] In Croatia there are two general regimes for entrepreneurs that are insolvent: the pre-bankruptcy proceeding and the bankruptcy proceeding in its two forms, ordinary and shortened. Both proceedings are covered by the same legislative act, the Bankruptcy Act (*Stečajni zakon* – Croatia official gazette nr. 71/15, 104/17).

[104] In addition, for companies of systemic importance for the Republic of Croatia there is an additional special proceeding, the extraordinary administration proceedings introduced and envisaged by the Act on the procedure of extraordinary administration in commercial companies of systemic importance for the Republic of Croatia (*Zakon o postupku izvanredne uprave u trgovačkim društvima od sistemskog značenja za Republiku Hrvatsku* – Croatian official gazette nr. 32/17).

[105] Companies of systemic importance are defined as joint-stock companies (*dionička društva*), excluding credit and financial institutions, which cumulatively meet the following criteria: (i) average of more than 5 000 employees in a calendar year, including its affiliated companies, and (ii) debt of more than HRK 7 500 000 000 (approx. EUR1 bn), including its affiliated companies.

[106] Pre-bankruptcy proceedings and extraordinary administration proceedings are primarily envisaged for the restructuring (financial and operational) and continuance of the debtor's operation; and while restructuring is also possible in bankruptcy proceedings, its main purpose is liquidating all the assets of a debtor.

[107] Directive (EU) 2019/1023 of the European Parliament and of the Council of 20 June 2019 on preventive restructuring frameworks, on discharge of debt and disqualifications, and on measures to increase the efficiency of procedures concerning restructuring, insolvency and discharge of debt, and amending Directive (EU) 2017/1132 (Directive on restructuring and insolvency) are implemented in Croatian legislation through the Bankruptcy Act.

10.2 Pre-bankruptcy

[108] The pre-bankruptcy proceeding is carried out in order to regulate the debtor's legal position and his relationship with creditors, as well as to structure/shape his inability to pay and maintain his business activities. The goal of the pre-bankruptcy procedure is to save the debtor from opening bankruptcy proceedings.

[109] In order to prevent the debtor's over-indebtedness, measures are proposed for the recovery of the debtor, i.e., a restructuring plan that seeks to extend the time for debt repayment or to write off part of the debt and thus avoid the possibility of opening bankruptcy proceedings.

[110] Pre-bankruptcy proceedings can be opened if the court determines that the debtor's ability to fulfil its due and existing obligations is threatened. This occurs if the petitioner makes it likely that the debtor will not be able to fulfil his existing obligations when due.

[111] The debtor's ability to fulfil due and existing obligations is assumed to be threatened if:

- there are unpaid payment orders in the Register of payment orders against the debtor,
- if the debtor is more than thirty days late with the payment of an employee's salary, or
- if the debtor does not pay contributions and taxes on the employee's salary within thirty days from the day he was obliged to pay the employee's salary.

[112] The existence of these circumstances can be proven by a certificate issued by the Financial Agency (FINA), which is under an obligation to issue such a certificate without delay at the request of the debtor or creditor.

[113] The debtor is authorized to submit a petition for the initiation of pre-bankruptcy proceedings. Along with the petition, the petitioner must submit financial statements not older than three months from the date of submission of the motion for opening bankruptcy proceedings, a statement of the number of employees on the last day of the month preceding the day of submission of the motion and a proposal for a restructuring plan, if it has been drawn up.

[114] Creditors in the pre-bankruptcy proceedings are 'personal' creditors of the debtor, i.e., those entities who, at the time of the opening of the pre-bankruptcy proceeding, have a property claim against the debtor. Creditors must report their claims against the debtor to FINA. Claims reported within the prescribed period are considered established if they have not been disputed by the debtor, trustee or creditor.

[115] The court will issue a decision on the conclusion of the pre-bankruptcy proceeding as soon as the decision on the confirmation of the restructuring plan becomes final. All established and contested claims must be included in the restructuring plan. The plan must contain an offer to creditors on the method, terms and conditions of settlement, the deadline for voluntary fulfilment and the amount of restructuring costs. Each group of creditors votes separately on the restructuring plan, and if they accept the plan with a majority of votes, the court will determine the acceptance of the restructuring plan and confirm the pre-bankruptcy agreement.

10.3 Bankruptcy

10.3.1 Effects of Commencing Insolvency Proceedings, Decision on Insolvency and Declaration of Bankruptcy

[116] Bankruptcy proceedings are carried out for the purpose of collective settlement of creditors of the debtor, by monetization of assets and distributing the collected funds to creditors. Bankruptcy proceedings may (and in some cases should) be initiated by either the debtor, creditors or the Croatian Financial Agency (FINA).

[117] Bankruptcy proceedings shall commence if one of the following conditions (bankruptcy reasons) is met:

(i) debtor's ability to fulfil due and existing obligations is threatened (*Prijeteća nesposobnost za plaćanje*), however only upon the debtor's request;
(ii) debtor's inability to fulfil due and existing obligations (*Nesposobnost za plaćanje*);
(iii) debtor is over-indebted (*Prezaduženost*).

[118] The request for opening of the bankruptcy proceeding can be submitted by the debtor or by the creditor:

- The debtor must submit the request for opening of the bankruptcy proceeding within twenty-one days from the day of occurrence of the bankruptcy reason.
- The Croatian financial agency must submit the request for opening of the bankruptcy proceeding against a legal entity if the legal entity in the Register of the order of payment title has had a record of unexecuted title for payment within an uninterrupted period of 120 days. In practice, this means that the legal entity would have its bank account blocked for a period of 120 days.

[119] If the legal entity has no employees, the Croatian Financial Agency may require the opening of a shortened bankruptcy proceeding. Then, if the persons authorized to represent the debtor by law do not submit a list of assets and liabilities of the debtor within fifteen days, or if the list shows that the debtor has assets that are insufficient to cover the foreseeable costs of bankruptcy proceedings and if no creditor within forty-five days proposes the opening of bankruptcy proceedings and does not advance funds to cover the costs of the proceedings, the debtor will be considered insolvent. And, in this case, the court will ex officio issue a decision on opening and concluding a shortened bankruptcy proceeding.

[120] The court will also issue a decision on opening and concluding a shortened bankruptcy proceeding where a request for opening of ordinary bankruptcy proceeding is submitted if, before the opening, the court determines that the assets would not be sufficient to cover the costs of the proceedings, or if its value is insignificant and no person having a legal interest for conduct of the bankruptcy proceeding has, upon public invitation, advanced the funds to cover the costs of the proceeding.

10.3.2 Avoidance Actinos – Claims of Preference or Creditor Prejudice

[121] Avoidance actions in cases of bankruptcy are regulated in detail by the Insolvency Act and these rules, by express provision of the law, apply also in case of extraordinary administration proceedings. For pre-bankruptcy proceedings the legislator has not expressly overruled or recalled the applicability of the rules governing the bankruptcy proceeding. Consequently, it is not clear if these rules or general rules provided for by the Croatian Obligations Act are applicable. However, there is a good argument to be made that avoidance actions should be applied in cases of pre-bankruptcy as well.

[122] Legal actions taken before the opening of bankruptcy proceedings, which disturb the right to uniform settlement of bankruptcy creditors (creditor prejudice) or which put individual bankruptcy creditors in a more favourable position (preference claims), may be challenged by bankruptcy creditors and the insolvency trustee on behalf of the bankruptcy debtor and in accordance with the provisions of the Insolvency Act. An omission due to which the bankruptcy debtor lost some right, or by which claims against the debtor arose, were maintained or secured, is also considered to be a 'legal action'.

Congruent Settlement

[123] Legal actions taken in the last three months prior to the filing of a motion for the opening of bankruptcy proceedings, which provides or enables a bankruptcy creditor to secure or settle in a manner and time in accordance with its right (congruent settlement), may be challenged if the debtor was insolvent and the creditor at the time knew of the insolvency.

[124] A legal action by which a bankruptcy creditor acquires security or settlement of its claim in accordance with the content of his right is voidable if it was taken after the submission of the motion for opening of the bankruptcy proceedings and if the creditor was aware of insolvency at the time of action or aware of the proposal for opening of the bankruptcy proceedings.

[125] The creditor will be deemed to have known of the insolvency or of the motion for opening of the bankruptcy proceeding if he was aware or should have been aware of the circumstances indicating the existence of insolvency, or that a motion for opening bankruptcy proceedings has been filed. A person close to the debtor at the time when the action was taken will be presumed to have been aware of the insolvency or the motion to open proceedings.

Non-congruent Settlement

[126] A legal action by which a bankruptcy creditor acquires security or settlement of its claim, which he did not have the right to demand or did not have the right to demand in that manner or at that time, may be challenged if:

(1) it was taken in the last month before or after the submission of the motion for opening of the bankruptcy proceeding; or
(2) if it was taken during the period of the third or second month before the submission of the motion for opening of bankruptcy proceedings, and at that time the debtor was incapable of making payment; or
(3) if the action was taken during the third or second month before the submission of the motion for opening bankruptcy proceedings, and the creditor was aware at the time of action that it causes damage to bankruptcy creditors.

Direct Prejudice to the Creditors

[127] A debtor's legal action by which the bankruptcy creditors are directly prejudiced may be challenged:

(1) if it was taken during the last three months before the submission of the motion for the opening of bankruptcy proceedings, if at that time the debtor was insolvent and the other party was aware of insolvency at that time; or
(2) if it was taken after the submission of the motion for opening bankruptcy proceedings, and the other party at the time of the legal transaction was aware or had to be aware about the insolvency or of the motion for opening bankruptcy proceedings.

Intentional Damage

[128] A legal action taken by a debtor in the period of the last ten years before or after submission of a proposal for opening bankruptcy proceedings with the intention of causing damage to the creditors may be challenged if the other party was aware of the debtor's intention at the time when the action was taken. Awareness is presumed if the other party knew that the debtor was threatened with insolvency and that the action would cause damage to the creditors. A contract with consideration concluded between a debtor and a close person may be contested if the bankruptcy creditors are directly damaged by it. The agreement cannot be contested if it was concluded earlier than two years before the submission of the motion for opening a bankruptcy proceeding or if the other party proves that it was not aware of the debtor's intention to damage creditors at the time of entering into the agreement.

A loan Which Replaces Capital

[129] Providing security or guaranteeing a shareholder loan granted in circumstances when the shareholder was supposed to provide capital can be contested:

- if the security was granted within the last five years before the submission of the proposal for opening bankruptcy proceedings or thereafter;
- if the loan is guaranteed, if the action was taken in the last year before or after the submission for the proposal for opening bankruptcy proceedings.

Silent Partnership

[130] Legal action by which the contribution of a secret member of the company is fully or partially reimbursed or by which his share in the loss is fully or partially forgiven is voidable, if the agreement on which the action is based was concluded in the last year before the proposal for opening of the bankruptcy proceedings against the company or thereafter. The same applies if the secret company is liquidated in connection with the agreement. Such legal action may not be challenged if the bankruptcy reason occurred only after the agreement.

10.3.3 The Bankruptcy Trustee

[131] The conditions for the appointment of a bankruptcy trustee in the pre-bankruptcy proceeding are the same as the preconditions for the appointment of a bankruptcy trustee in the bankruptcy proceeding. A person can be appointed as an insolvency trustee, if he/she is listed on the official list of insolvency trustees for the area of the competent court. The trustee's duties in case of a pre-bankruptcy proceeding are to:

(1) Examine the debtor's business.
(2) Examine the list of assets and liabilities of the debtor.
(3) Examine the credibility of the reported claims.
(4) Dispute the claims if based on a statement from a creditor or if for some other reason he suspects their existence.
(5) Supervise the debtor's operations, in particular financial operations by the debtor, creation of obligations towards third parties, issuance of means of payment security, and conduct of business in the sale of goods and services, ensuring that the debtor's assets are not damaged.
(6) File a complaint with the court if the debtor acts contrary to the provisions of the Insolvency Act.
(7) Issue orders and certificates in accordance with the provisions of the Insolvency Act.
(8) Monitor the timely and due payment of costs of the pre-bankruptcy proceedings.
(9) Perform other tasks in accordance with the Insolvency Act.

[132] The trustee in the bankruptcy proceeding has the duties and authorities of corporate bodies of the debtor as a legal person. If the debtor continues to operate during the bankruptcy proceedings the business is run by the trustee. The trustee's duties are to:

(1) bring in order the register of bookkeeping up to the date of opening bankruptcy proceedings;
(2) draw up an estimate of the costs of the bankruptcy proceedings and submit it for the approval of the creditors committee;
(3) appoint a committee for listing the assets of the debtor;
(4) prepare the initial balance of the debtor's assets;
(5) take care of the initiated but uncompleted business of the debtor and of the business needed to prevent the occurrence of the damage to the debtor's assets;
(6) take care of the realization of the debtor's claim;
(7) conscientiously conduct the business of the debtor in case of continuance;
(8) submit documents to the Croatian Pension Insurance Institute relating to the employment status of any insured person;
(9) cash the assets and rights of debtors entering the bankruptcy estate;
(10) prepare the payment of creditors and, after approval, make the relevant payments;
(11) submit to the committee of creditors the final invoice;
(12) perform subsequent payments of the creditors;
(13) after completion of the bankruptcy proceeding represent the bankruptcy estate.

10.3.4 The Court (*dodao sam ovaj dio o sudu, činilo mi se bitnim*)

[133] The court in the bankruptcy proceedings has the following competences (art. 76 of the Insolvency Act):

(1) decides on initiating a preliminary proceeding for the purpose of determining the existence of a bankruptcy ground and conducts that proceeding;
(2) decides on the opening of bankruptcy proceedings;
(3) appoints and dismisses the insolvency trustee, supervises his work and gives him mandatory instructions, in accordance with the Insolvency Act;
(4) oversees the work of the Creditors' committee;
(5) determines the started business to be completed during the bankruptcy proceeding, in accordance with the Insolvency Act;
(6) determines the award to the insolvency trustee;
(7) approves the payment of the creditor;
(8) makes decisions on concluding and suspending bankruptcy proceedings;
(9) decides on all other issues of bankruptcy proceedings, if under the Insolvency Act, those issues are not to be decided by some other body of the bankruptcy proceeding.

10.3.5 Creditors' Committee

[134] To protect the interests of creditors in bankruptcy proceedings, the court may establish a creditors' committee and appoint its members before the first hearing of creditors. There must be an odd number of members of the creditors' committee, and a maximum of ten. The creditors' committee supervises the bankruptcy trustee and assists him in managing his affairs, monitors the course of business, fulfilment of which is necessary to prevent damage to the bankruptcy debtor, reviews business books and business documentation, and orders a check of turnover and the amount of cash.

[135] The highest ranked creditors (regular creditors) and those with lower rank of claims (subordinated creditors) must be represented in the creditors committee. A representative of the debtor's former employees should also be represented on the creditors committee unless they participate in the proceeding as creditors with insignificant claims.

[136] Secured creditors (*razlučni vjerovnici*) and persons who are not creditors may also be appointed as members of the creditors committee if they could contribute to the work of that board with their professional knowledge. If the number of bankruptcy creditors is less than five, all creditors shall have the powers of the creditors committee.

10.3.6 Creditors' Assembly

[137] The creditors' assembly is convened by the court, and all bankruptcy creditors have the right to participate. The assembly of creditors can:

(i) Establish a creditors' committee, if it has not been established, or change its composition or abolish it.
(ii) Appoint a new insolvency trustee.
(iii) Decide on the operations of the debtor; and on the conditions for cashing out those assets that are not encumbered by separate law.
(iv) Order the bankruptcy trustee to draw up a bankruptcy plan.
(v) Make all decisions within the jurisdiction of the creditors' committee.

10.3.7 Distribution of Assets: Priority Claims and Ranking

[138] The bankruptcy estate includes all assets of the debtor at the time of opening the bankruptcy proceedings and the assets acquired by the debtor during the bankruptcy proceedings. The bankruptcy estate serves to settle the costs of the bankruptcy proceedings and the claims of the creditors of the bankrupt debtor. As a general rule, bankruptcy creditors are ranked in order for payment according to their claims. Creditors of lower payment rank cannot be settled until the creditors from the previous rank have been completely settled. Creditors of the same payment rank will be settled proportionally to their claims

[139] Claims are ranked as follows:

(1) bankruptcy estate – claims of the bankruptcy estate include bankruptcy proceedings costs and other claims of the bankruptcy estate (attorney claims etc.);
(2) creditors with right of separation (*Izlučni vjerovnici*) – they may request extraction of objects to which they are entitled out of the bankruptcy estate;
(3) secured creditors (*Razlučni vjerovnici*) – their claims are satisfied from secured assets;
(4) regular bankruptcy creditors (*Viši isplatni red*) – unsubordinated and unsecured creditors whose claims are classified into ranks depending on the particular claim as follows:
   - first rank – claims of employees and of former employees arising from employment and certain related claims;
   - second rank – other general claims against the debtor, except for the subordinated claims
(5) subordinated bankruptcy creditors (*Niži isplatni red*).

[140] In the pre-bankruptcy proceeding, the claim must be lodged with the FINA on the prescribed form and contain the following:

(1) creditor identification data;
(2) debtor identification data;
(3) legal basis of the claim, the amount of the due claim and the amount of the claim due after the opening of the pre-bankruptcy proceedings in HRK countervalue;
(4) an indication of the proof of the existence of the claim;
(5) an indication of the existence of an enforcement document.

[141] Lodging of the claim must be accompanied by documents from which the claim arises. The court will reject any application submitted after the expiry of the application deadline, i.e., twenty-nine days from the day of publication on the website of the court '*e-oglasna ploča*'. The court will also reject the application if it is not filed on the prescribed form.

[142] In the bankruptcy proceeding, the claim must be lodged with the FINA on the prescribed form and contain the following:

(1) creditor identification data;
(2) debtor identification data;
(3) legal basis of the claim, the amount of the due in HRK countervalue;
(4) an indication of the proof of the existence of the claim;
(5) an indication of the existence of an enforcement document;
(6) an indication of the existence of proceedings before the court.

[143] Lodging of the claim must be accompanied by the documents from which the claim arises, i.e., by which it is proved in the transcript.

[144] In the extraordinary administration proceedings, the claim must be lodged with the extraordinary trustee within a mandatory deadline of sixty days from the day of publication of the decision on opening of the bankruptcy proceedings on the website of the court, '*e-oglasna ploča*'.

11 CHOICE OF LAW

11.1 Choice of Law

[145] The choice of a foreign law to govern an agreement entered into by a Croatian party will be valid under the conditions stipulated by Regulation (EC) No. 593/2008 of the European Parliament and of the Council of 17 June 2008 on the Law Applicable to Contractual Obligations (Rome I). Choice of law is also recognized by Croatian Private International Law Act (OG 101/17), which applies in so far as Rome I or other EU or international documents are not applicable.

[146] It is recommended that agreements relating to assets registered in public registers (real estate, ownership interest in a limited liability company) or rights to be entered into public registers or a notarial register (e.g., fixed or floating charges of assets situated in Croatia) be governed by Croatian law.

11.2 Jurisdiction

[147] Judgments obtained in other member countries of the European Union are enforceable in Croatia in line with Regulation No. 1215/2012 of the European Parliament and of the Council of 12 December 2012 on jurisdiction and the recognition and enforcement of judgments in civil and commercial matters and the Private International Law Act.

[148] The Hague Convention on Choice of Court Agreements is effective in Croatia from 1 October 2015.

[149] Under general statutory regulations, a decision of a foreign court will not be recognized and enforced in the Croatia, for example, if:

(a) the matter is one that is within the exclusive jurisdiction of the Croatian courts or other Croatian authority; or
(b) the jurisdiction of the foreign court was established exclusively on the basis of presence of the defendant or its assets in the foreign country, where such presence is not directly connected to matter in dispute; or
(c) the jurisdiction of the court was established contrary to section II, Chapters 3, 4 or 5 of Regulation No. 1215/2012;

(d) a final decision on the same matter between the same parties has previously been reached by a competent Croatian court or a recognized or recognizable prior final decision of a foreign court has been rendered; or
(e) recognition of the foreign judgment would be clearly contrary to the public policy; or
(f) the party against whom the enforcement of such judgment is sought has been deprived of the opportunity to participate in the foreign proceedings.

11.3 Arbitration

[150] An arbitral award or decision of an arbitral tribunal will be recognized and enforced in Croatia in accordance with, and subject to, the New York Convention on Recognition and Enforcement of Foreign Arbitral Awards made in New York on 10 June 1958 and the Private International Law Act.

12 MOST COMMON ACQUISITION TRANSACTIONS

12.1 Types of Transactions

[151] The most commonly used acquisition transactions are:

(a) the acquisition of shares in a joint-stock company;
(b) the acquisition of an ownership interest in a limited liability company;
(c) the acquisition of company's assets; and

In practice, (a) and (b) are usually referred to as 'share deals' and (c) as 'asset deals'.

12.2 General Information

[152] The parties are free to determine the rights and obligations of the acquisition agreement as they see fit, as long as mandatory provisions of Croatian law are not thereby violated. In addition, various procedural requirements apply to each of these acquisition methods. The number and type of procedural requirements that must be fulfilled in order to carry out the selected acquisition method should also be considered with respect to timing and indirect acquisition costs in particular. From a procedural point of view, the acquisition of shares in a joint-stock company or an ownership interest in a limited liability company or the acquisition of assets are the least complicated, while the acquisition of an enterprise (or a part thereof) require more procedural steps be taken.

[153] During negotiations, it is quite common for the parties to execute a letter of intent or a memorandum of understanding setting out certain terms of the transaction. Under certain circumstances, a party could be liable for damages, if it unjustifiably terminated the negotiations. In general, such damages are limited to direct losses but would not include loss of profits.

12.3 Transfer of Liabilities

[154] The biggest difference between 'share deals' and 'asset deals' is in the transfer of liabilities.

[155] In cases of share deals, the target is a company. As a consequence, the company is acquired together with all its existing assets and liabilities. For that reason, extinguishing of certain liabilities (e.g., a liability of the target to the selling shareholders) is often a condition precedent for completion of a share deal.

[156] By contrast, in the case of an asset deal, as a general rule the liabilities do not transfer. However, there are exceptions. By way of an example, a person acquiring by contract an economic unit (enterprise, etc.) of a legal entity, or a part of that unit, is jointly and severally liable for debts related to the acquired economic unit (or to that part thereof) together with the seller, but only up to the value of the acquired assets.

12.4 Representations and Warranties

[157] The concept of representations and warranties and the consequences of their breach are not explicitly regulated under Croatian law. Notwithstanding this fact, representations and warranties can frequently be found in contractual clauses in agreements governed by Croatian law.

[158] Nevertheless, to offset this insecurity, the parties often opt for a foreign law governed 'purchase agreement' and Croatian law governed 'transfer agreement'. Purchase agreements governed by foreign law (in cases where this is practicable and legally possible) set out in detail the rights and obligations of the parties. The transfer agreement is often a short document, of a page or two, whereby the parties simply agree for the transfer of the shares/assets to take place and allow for registration of the transfer in relevant registers.

12.5 Acquisition of Shares in a Joint-stock Company

12.5.1 Transfer of Shares

[159] The method of transferring title to the shares depends on the type of share that is being transferred.

[160] The title to all types of shares is transferred on the basis of a share purchase agreement (SPA) and conditions set out for transfer in such SPA.

[161] In the case of a transfer of shares issued in physical form, ownership of bearer shares may be transferred by simple delivery of the document. Paper shares can also be transferred by endorsement. Articles of Association may require the consent of the company itself (given by the management board) for the transfer of paper shares. However, only a person who is registered in the share register will be considered a shareholder.

[162] In the case of a transfer of book-entered shares, these are transferred by crediting them to the account of the acquirer held by the Central Depository and Clearing Company.

[163] In practice, shares in joint-stock companies are in most, if not all, cases held in electronic form. Hence, the relevant time of transfer will be when they are credited to the account of the acquirer held by the Central Clearing and Depository Company.

[164] The acquirer acquires the shares when they are credited to the account of the acquirer (or the person holding the shares for the acquirer – e.g., a custodian).

12.5.2 Consequences of the Acquisition of Shares

[165] The acquisition of regular shares has, in particular, the following consequences:

(a) The buyer is entitled to vote at the general meeting of the company.
(b) The buyer is entitled to receive dividends, if declared.
(c) In case of liquidation, the buyer is entitled to receive a part of any remaining assets of the wound up company.
(d) The buyer of shares listed for trading on stock exchanges may have various reporting duties regarding the number of shares held by the buyer and also by entities acting in concert with the buyer. Furthermore, it may, upon exceeding certain thresholds, be obliged to carry out a mandatory takeover procedure.
(e) The buyer acquires a shareholding in the company with all public law licences and permits issued to the company. If the company has any such licences or permits, the acquisition may be subject to the notification and/or approval of the relevant authorities.
(f) The buyer becomes liable to pay up any outstanding capital contribution related to the shares, in breach of which it can be expelled from the company. The seller is, by operation of law, a guarantor of the expelled buyer's obligation to pay up the shares.
(g) The buyer is not liable for any other liabilities of the joint-stock company, unless it abuses the corporate shield/veil, in which case it can become subject to piercing of the corporate shield.

12.5.3 Issues to Be Considered in Share Deals

[166]

(a) The possible use of the assets of the acquired joint-stock company as security for financing the acquisition is limited if the transaction is regarded as constituting the provision of 'financial assistance' by the target company.
(b) The cash flow generated by the assets of the target joint-stock company, as well as any proceeds arising from the sale of the target joint-stock company's assets, accrue to the target joint-stock company itself. Financing an acquisition through such cash flow could be considered to be contrary to capital maintenance. Hence, any payments from the target to the buyer should be based only on declared dividends or on payments arising out of arm's length contracts between the buyer and the target.
(c) Although contracts binding on the target joint-stock company generally remain in force, the potential buyer should be aware of any possible termination clauses in such contracts entitling the counterparty to terminate the contract in the event of any change of control. Such termination clauses are, for example, common in financing arrangements.
(d) A buyer of less than 100% of the shares in a joint-stock company should verify: (i) the level of the various majority requirements for adopting decisions of the target joint-stock company's general meeting, so that it can plan the purchase of the number shares required to effectively control the joint-stock company, and (ii) the rights of the remaining minority shareholders.

12.5.4 Squeeze-Out with Transfer of Shares to the Majority Shareholder

[167] The Business Corporations Act allows a shareholder or shareholders who own shares representing at least 95% of the share capital in a joint-stock company the right to enforce the transfer of the shares of the remaining shareholders to it for fair compensation.

[168] The squeeze-out procedure involves, in particular, the following steps:

(a) Check that the majority shareholder(s) holds at least 95% of the share capital.
(b) Request the Management Board the necessary documents to quantify the value of the shares and the amount to be offered as compensation.
(c) Appoint a technical expert to quantify the amount that the majority shareholder must request and deposit, before the meeting, subject to a guarantee issued by the Bank.
(d) Request from the competent Court the appointment of an expert to check the appropriateness of the cash compensation.
(e) Deposit of the documents necessary to convene the general meeting.
(f) Convocation of the general meeting of shareholders.
(g) General meeting decision on the share transfer proposal.

(h) Registration of the share transfer resolution in the commercial register.
(i) Transfer of the minority shares to the principal shareholder, upon the registration of the Transfer Resolution in the Commercial Register.
(j) Within two months of registration, if the compensation is not paid or is claimed to be inadequate, the minority shareholders are entitled to claim the cash compensation and to ask the competent court to recalculate it.
(k) If the Court determines that the amount of the Cash Compensation set by the principal shareholder is inadequate, the principal shareholder is required to pay the compensation determined by the Court.

12.6 Acquisition of an Ownership Interest in a Limited Liability Company

[169] An ownership interest in a limited liability company is not represented by securities. Therefore, different rules apply to its transfer in comparison with shares in a joint-stock company.

[170] In practice, the parties will first sign a SPA. The SPA must be in writing, in the form of a notarial deed. The SPA may, but need not, contain a clause authorising the transfer of shares. If it does, the transfer can be carried out on the basis of the SPA. However, the SPA will often contain certain conditions precedent which need to be fulfilled before a separate share transfer agreement (STA) is signed. In such cases, the share transfer will be implemented on the basis of the STA.

[171] If the SPA is signed outside Croatia, an apostille or superlegalization may be required. Parties sometimes sign an SPA without notarization. If, following the SPA, the parties sign an STA in the form of a notarial deed, this will rectify any lack of form of the SPA. However, if the parties do not agree and do not sign a share transfer agreement, an SPA not signed in the appropriate form may be unenforceable.

[172] Either an SPA or an STA, depending on the agreement of the parties, must contain a clause expressly allowing for share transfer and the registration of such transfer, a clause sometimes called *clausula intabulandi*.

[173] On the basis of *clausula intabulandi*, the following is required for the share transfer to be fully effected:

- the management of the company must register the share transfer in the share register maintained by the company;
- submission to the commercial court register of a list of shareholders by the target management (in practice this is done by the notary public, who will at the closing collect all necessary signatures and documents).

[174] The transfer of an ownership interest to another shareholder does not require the approval of the target's corporate bodies, unless the need for such approval is explicitly stipulated in the articles of association. The memorandum of association may contain additional restrictions on the transfer of an ownership interest.

12.7 Acquisition of Assets

12.7.1 General

[175] In an asset purchase transaction, the assets (tangible and/or intangible), are transferred individually and each must be precisely specified in the transaction documentation.

[176] In legal theory, an enterprise or a part of an enterprise can also be transferred. An enterprise is deemed to be constituted by the aggregate of debts and assets which the entrepreneur has created and which serve the operation of the enterprise. Given that an enterprise comprises both assets and liabilities it can also have a negative value. However, the transfer of an enterprise is in practice done in the same manner as an asset transfer.

12.7.2 Specification of Assets and Liabilities

[177] The exact specification of all the assets (both tangible and intangible) to be transferred is vital for the enforceability of the asset transfer agreement. Where a large numbers of assets are to be transferred, the individual assets are usually listed in an annex to the transfer agreement. In addition, there may be an interim period between the signing of the agreement and completion and, therefore, it may be necessary to stipulate that the list of assets in the annex is subject to change in the normal course of business. A provision for the disclosure of the completion accounts would be the normal method of assessing and identifying the state of the assets upon completion.

[178] In cases where the assets to be transferred contain real property or other assets the ownership of which is registered in the relevant registers, and subject to specific form, separate transfer agreements for such assets may need to be executed in the requisite form (e.g., signature certified by a notary) and registered in the relevant register (e.g., land register).

12.7.3 Acquired Liabilities

[179] As previously mentioned, in cases where an enterprise or a part of an enterprise is purchased, the buyer is jointly and severally liable for debts related to the acquired enterprise (or its part) together with the seller, but only up to the value of the acquired assets.

[180] In addition, in case of the transfer of an enterprise or a part of an enterprise, the employment contracts of all employees who work in the enterprise continue in force with the purchaser as part of the transfer.

13 SPECIFIC RULES ON PUBLIC TAKEOVERS

13.1 General

[181] In Croatia, public takeovers have been regulated since 1997 by the Law on Takeover of joint-stock companies ('Takeover Act') which was ultimately amended in 2013. Public offers are not frequently used to acquire control in Croatia. According to the Croatian Financial Services supervisory agency ('Agency'), in 2022 there were only three published takeover offers for the following companies: *OT-OPTIMA TELEKOM d.d.*, *ŽITNJAK proizvodnja i promet robom d.d.*, and *TANKERSKA NEXT GENERATION d.d.*

13.2 Obligation to Publish Takeover Bid

[182] An entity controls another legal entity if it has:

- directly or indirectly more than a 25% share in the share capital of the relevant legal entity;
- directly or indirectly more than 25% of the voting rights in the general meeting of the legal entity;
- the right to manage the business and financial policies of the legal entity on the basis of authority from statute or an agreement; or
- direct or indirect dominant influence on the management of the business and decision-making.

[183] The main principles which govern the Takeover Act are the following:

- shareholders of the target company, who hold shares of the target company of the same class, to which the takeover offer refers, have an equal position in the takeover process;
- the shareholders of the target company to whom the takeover offer applies must have enough time and information to be able to decide on the takeover offer with a complete insight into its state of affairs;
- the board of directors and supervisory board of the target company are obliged to act in the best interests of the target company during the period of the takeover procedure;
- the bidder and the target company are obliged to carry out the takeover procedure as quickly as possible, and the target company must not be prevented from doing business for any longer time than planned.

[184] A natural or legal person is obliged to publish a takeover offer when, directly or indirectly, independently or acting jointly, they acquire voting shares of the target company which, together with the shares already held, exceed the threshold of 25% of the voting shares of the target.

13.3 Financial Aspects

[185] A joint-stock company is prohibited from providing financial assistance for the purpose of financing the acquisition of its shares. The joint-stock company may not repay shareholder contributions. Furthermore, all payments to shareholders are prohibited, with the exception of dividends from net profits approved by the general meeting and those arising out of arm's length contracts.

13.4 Duties of the Board of Directors

[186] The board of directors has to publish its reasoned opinion on the takeover offer, which must contain inter alia, an opinion on the following: the type and amount of compensation offered, the intentions of the bidder regarding the future business plans of the target company, strategic plans of the bidder in relation to the target company, as well as any possible changes to the places where the company carries on its activities, etc. The reasoned opinion must be delivered to the Agency, and if it contains false or misleading information, the board of directors will be liable for damages if they knew or ought to have known that this information was false or misleading.

[187] Moreover, after the notification of the takeover offer has been published, the board of directors and supervisory board of the target company may not, without the approval of the general assembly of the target company, increase the share capital, enter into transactions outside the regular operations of the target company, act in a way that could seriously threaten the further operations of the target company or enter into deals that could seriously threaten the further operations of the target company, decide on the acquisition and disposal of the target company's own shares (or securities giving the right to those shares) nor act in any way having the aim of disrupting or preventing a takeover offer.

[188] This provision has been criticized by the Croatian jurisprudence, as it is considered as a provision advocating a neutral position on the part of the board of directors.

14 OTHER RELEVANT LAWS, ANTI-BRIBERY

14.1 Anti-bribery Laws

[189] Pursuant to the Croatian Criminal Code, a bribe means any undue reward, gift or other pecuniary or non-pecuniary benefit, regardless of value ('Bribe'). Crimes of corruption might also be committed by a company (*see* below in paragraph **[195]**). There are several criminal offences prescribed by Criminal Code regarding bribery:

(i) **Accepting bribery** – an official or a responsible person who demands or receives a bribe, or who accepts an offer or promise of a bribe for himself or another to carry out an official or other action within or beyond the limits of his jurisdiction that should not be carried out, or to refrain from carrying out an official or other action that should be carried out. The maximum sentence is ten years imprisonment. The crime becomes statute-barred after twenty years.
(ii) **Trading in influence** – Whoever demands or receives a bribe or accepts an offer or promise of a bribe for himself or another, to use his official or social position or influence to mediate the performance of an official or other action that should not be performed, or not to perform an official or other action that ought to be done. The maximum sentence is ten years imprisonment. The crime becomes statute-barred after twenty years.
(iii) **Giving bribes in order to trade in influence** – whoever offers, promises or gives a bribe to another person, intended for that or another person, to use his or her official or social position or influence to mediate the performance of an official or other action that should not be performed or not to perform an official or other action that Ought to be done. The maximum sentence is ten years imprisonment. The crime becomes statute-barred after five years.

[190] It follows from the above that bribery is considered to be a crime regardless of whether the bribe was given/offered to a public official or whether it was given/offered in a business transaction between two private individuals/companies. However, the most frequently prosecuted cases still relate to the bribery of public officials.

[191] Police and state prosecutors are persistent in their efforts to fight corruption. In this light several high-profile criminal prosecutions relating to bribery (involving several top politicians) have been initiated.

[192] In addition, the 'long reach' of the United States' Foreign Corrupt Practices Act (FCPA) or the United Kingdom (UK) Bribery Act has an effect on M&A transactions, as foreign investors often undertake anti-bribery due diligence before acquiring a Croatian target (especially if the target operates in a risky sector, such as the construction industry).

14.2 Act on the Criminal Liability of Legal Entities

14.2.1 General Information

[193] The Liability of Legal Persons for Criminal Offences Act ('Act') was adopted in 2003 and finally amended in 2012.

[194] The Act determines the presumptions of criminality, penalties, security measures, confiscation of material benefits, confiscation of objects, public announcement of the verdict, statute of limitations and criminal procedure for criminal offences of legal persons.

14.2.2 'Attributability' of Acts Committed by Certain Individuals to a Legal Entity

[195] A legal person will be punished for the criminal offence of the responsible person if it violates a duty of the legal person, or the legal person has achieved or should have achieved an illegal financial benefit for itself or another. A responsible person within the meaning of the Act is a natural person who manages the affairs of a legal entity or is entrusted with the performance of affairs in the field of activity of a legal person. The liability of a legal entity is based on guilt of a responsible person.

14.2.3 Exemption from Punishment

[196] A legal entity that reports a criminal offence to a responsible person prior to its discovery, or before learning that the offence has been discovered, may be exempted from punishment.

14.2.4 Succession of Criminal Liability to Legal Successors

[197] The criminal liability of a legal person passes to its legal successors. When considering the punishment for each of the successors, the competent court will consider the extent to which the benefits from the relevant crime or crimes passed to such successor.

14.2.5 Sanctions

[198] The penalties for legal persons are fines and termination of the legal person. Protective measures can also be prescribed against legal persons. Protective measures include the prohibition of carrying out certain activities or jobs, prohibition of obtaining permits, authorizations, concessions or subsidies, prohibition of doing business with beneficiaries of the state and local budgets, and confiscation of items.

[199] Legal persons may commit any criminal offence prescribed by the Criminal Code except criminal offences which can be committed only by natural persons.

14.2.6 Enforcement Trends

[200] Ever since the Act has been adopted, Croatia has seen a constant rise of companies convicted for criminal offences.

14.3 Money-laundering Regulations

[201] Money laundering is regulated by the Act on the Prevention of Money Laundering and Terrorist Financing (the AML Act), which implements EU Directive No. 2015/849. The AML Act stipulates certain obligations for financial institutions but also some other persons/entities dealing with transactions (such as attorneys or notaries when handling escrow payments). For all transactions exceeding EUR1 000, the AML Act stipulates an obligation to identify the client. If the value of the transaction exceeds EUR15 000, a customer due diligence must be performed. The AML Act also stipulates a reporting obligation in respect of suspicious transactions (e.g., unusually large transactions, or transactions without apparent economic or visible lawful purpose).

[202] The AML Act also prohibits (with certain exceptions) cash payments exceeding EUR10 000.00).

[203] Money laundering is defined as:

(1) conversion or transfer of property, when it is known that the property has been derived from criminal activity or participation in such activity, for the purpose of concealing or disguising the illicit origin of the property, or of assisting any person involved in the commission of such activity to evade the legal consequences of actions taken by that person;
(2) concealment or disguise of the true nature, source, location, disposition, movement, rights with respect to, or ownership of, property, knowing that such property has been derived from criminal activity or from participation in such activity;
(3) acquisition, possession or use of property, knowing, at the time of receipt, that such property has been derived from criminal activity or from participation in such activity;
(4) participation in, association to commit, attempts to commit, and aiding, abetting, facilitating or counselling the commission of any of the activities referred to in items 1, 2 and 3 above, when someone receives, transfers or transports abroad, or assists in the transfer of title or possession of legal tender, securities or other foreign currency values, property rights or real or movable property obtained from the profits of offences committed by other people, or takes any other action that may prevent or significantly hinder the determination of their criminal origin or place of location, their detection or forfeiture.

15 THE DUE DILIGENCE PROCESS

15.1 General Introduction

[204] Due diligence usually begins once the buyer has already examined the general information on the target available in public documents and agreed with the seller on a tentative price for the deal. At this stage, the purchaser normally engages external advisors to assess legal, financial, technical, and the environmental position of the target.

[205] The milestones that typically mark the official onset of due diligence process are the signing of a confidentiality agreement and of a letter of intent, (or heads of terms) in which the parties, inter alia, outline the rules for the due diligence process and agree on the time allowed/available for due diligence. Purchasers are sometimes granted exclusivity for negotiations with the seller for a certain period of time. Exclusivity agreements are regularly seen in cases where the purchaser has submitted a preliminary non-binding offer based on initial information provided by the seller in the information memorandum and the parties have agreed to negotiate the deal further based on such preliminary offer.

[206] Information on the target is typically disclosed in virtual data rooms (VDR). International companies and sellers regularly set up professional virtual data rooms which are regulated by confidentiality and non-disclosure rules binding on all persons granted access to the VDR. Smaller local companies are generally not ready to commit to setting up a professional VDRs and would likely go for free of charge data rooms (e.g., Dropbox, Google Drive) or would deliver the requested information in physical form. Physical data rooms are seen very rarely in the last couple of years. In larger deals, a physical data room may be prepared after the purchaser has already been given a chance to review the information on a target disclosed in the VDR, for a part of the target's documentation that requires additional investigation.

[207] Legal due diligence covers all relevant legal relations of a target, validity of existing agreements, and other legal matters that must be clarified so that a final decision in respect of the acquisition can be taken. Comprehensive due diligence is almost entirely abandoned. 'Red flag' due diligence has predominated in the last couple of years, irrespective of the size of a deal.

[208] Even though due diligence is substantially based on documents provided by the seller, information from public registers must also be reviewed as in most deals disclosure would include all information on the target that was published in public registers at the time of the due diligence process (unless explicitly excluded in transaction documents). There is a range of public registers searchable online such as the Commercial Registry, Land Registry, Intellectual Property Registry, Ship Registry, Financial Agency's Pledges on Movables and Rights Registry ('FINA's Registry'), Renewable Energy Projects Registry, Concessions Registry etc. While most of these registers would give accurate information, purchasers should consider keeping only information searchable at online versions of Commercial Registry and Land Registry within the definition of 'disclosure' usually applicable to transaction documents. All other online registers can prove unreliable in many cases as they cannot be properly searched by entering only the basic information on registration (e.g., company name, Croatian Personal Identification Number and similar). This is especially the case with FINA's Registry which sometimes requires that all relevant details on any particular registration be entered into the searching tool to provide accurate results.

15.2 Specific Issues to Be Reviewed

[209] If a target is a Croatian company which has undergone the privatization process, or has acquired assets from another company which has undergone privatization, legal due diligence should inspect the accuracy of the privatization process and verify whether there are any existing or threatened claims which are or might be raised with respect to the target's shares or assets. The Croatian privatization process is characterized by somewhat vague laws and sluggishness on the part of the privatization authorities. Consequently, privatization of many Croatian companies has simply been done wrong. Some privatization processes are being revised even today by courts within litigation or administrative dispute proceedings in which the State (as legal successor of the former Croatian Privatization Fund) claims ownership over shares or assets in fully privatized companies.

[210] Privatization-related issues are particularly common in case of companies operating hotel and camp properties on the Croatian coast. During the privatization process of former social enterprises (*Cro. društvena poduzeća*) hotel buildings were evaluated and contributed to the share capital of a privatized company but the land under and around the hotel buildings (which is nowadays mostly used for camps) was not. After the privatization process, the hotel buildings, by virtue of law, became the property of the privatized company, and the land under and around the buildings became the property of the Republic of Croatia. However, hotel operators continued to utilize the land, without paying regard to the State. There were several attempts by the State to resolve the ambiguities surrounding the property rights over the land surrounding hotel buildings (the last being the Act on Non-Evaluated Construction Land), however, none of them came to life. Many companies still do not have clearly regulated property relations for land surrounding the hotel buildings and are engaged in heavyweight long-term disputes with the State before Croatian courts.

[211] In the case of Croatian targets which acquired real properties that were previously under the social ownership regime, the critical area of due diligence is to verify whether the real property in question is subject to any claims for return of property confiscated under the Yugoslav Communist Rule. Restitution claims should have been submitted by 7 January 2003, as a result of which most have been resolved by now. However, some restitution proceedings might still be pending due to stays of restitution proceedings or annulment of lower instance decisions. The existence or otherwise of restitution claims can be verified based on the official confirmation issued by competent state administration offices which keep the register of all restitution claims in Croatia.

[212] Given the current geopolitical and economic situation with the ongoing war in Ukraine, a new critical issue that will be covered by legal due diligence of any Croatian targets owned by Russian entities or citizens, is the sanctions against Russia imposed by the EU, Office of Foreign Assets Control (OFAC) and UK. Thus far, due diligence efforts on this issue have mostly focused on independent checks of public corporate and UBO registers and on verifying whether the entities and persons in the chain of ownership behind the Croatian target are listed on one of the sanction's lists.

15.3 Disclosure Restrictions

15.3.1 General

[213] Generally, even a majority shareholder is not entitled to instruct the target company to provide any information to a third party (purchaser) for the purpose of a due diligence review, unless it is allowed to do so under the Articles of Association of the relevant target company. This is especially the case for targets which are joint-stock companies (*Cro. dioničko društvo*) where the decision-making processes of the management board are strictly separated from those of the general assembly (formed of all shareholders) of a company. There is no law under which a target would be required to allow the bidder to perform a due diligence, however, the target's management may permit a due diligence by the bidder if this would be in the target's best interest. Therefore, any due diligence process requires cooperation with the representatives of both the seller and the target company as the representatives of the target company are solely responsible for its business management and operations and are obliged to act in the best interests of the target company.

[214] The purchaser will normally enter into a confidentiality agreement with the target company committing itself to comply with security measures adopted by the target company to avoid the abuse or disclosure of information made available to the purchaser in the course of the due diligence. Such measures are commonly set out in the confidentiality or non-disclosure agreement (NDA) concluded between the target company and the purchaser, and in the form of binding (virtual) data room rules also containing confidentiality undertakings which need to be accepted by all persons which have been granted access to the (virtual) data room or to specific sections of the VDR. Most VDRs contain additional security measures such as automatic log-off if the user is inactive for a certain period; keeping a record of the history of use of the data room by a given user (i.e., dates and times of access; reviewed documents); and whether printing will be permitted or not, (and/or for which portion of documents). In the case of large-scale transactions, so-called clean teams are sometimes established – access to sensitive information being granted only to the members of a clean team, usually based on a separate non-disclosure agreement with each member of that clean team.

15.3.2 Business Secrets

[215] A business secret includes information that is not commonly available or known in business circles and that its holder wishes or needs to maintain confidential. In the course of a due diligence, a purchaser and its advisers will usually encounter business secrets of the target company, as well as business secrets of persons and entities in contractual (or other) relationships with the target company.

[216] It is at the sole discretion of the target company whether or not business secrets will be disclosed to the purchaser and to decide the terms and conditions for such disclosure. This freedom of disclosure is not absolute as the parties are still bound by restrictions imposed by competition law prohibiting the exchange of sensitive commercial information between competitors in a manner that could lead to distortion of fair competition, or to the effective integration of businesses before competition authority merger clearance has been granted (no 'gun jumping'). To prevent the possibilities of unallowed exchange of sensitive commercial information leading to breach of competition law obligations of the parties, a number of methods have been developed to allow for meaningful disclosure in the course of the due diligence process – similar to those generally described under section [214].

[217] In relation to information classified as a business secret by third parties, the target company must ensure a level of protection corresponding to the scope of protection it has agreed to provide to the relevant third party, unless the third-party consents to the required data disclosure.

15.3.3 Personal Data Protection

[218] Personal data means any information relating to an identified or identifiable individual, defined as a 'data subject' (applicable only to data of natural persons). The target company is only entitled to disclose personal data upon the relevant data subject's consent or in cases where an exemption is stipulated by the General Data Protection Regulation.

[219] There is no explicit exemption for the disclosure of personal data within the scope of due diligence. However, the prevailing view is that such disclosure is allowed, provided that the disclosure is essential for the protection of the rights of the target company. Anonymization, pseudonymization and aggregation of personal data are commonly used as measures of protection of personal data through due diligence processes.

15.3.4 Banking Secrets

[220] Under the Credit Institutions Act, all data, facts and circumstances of which the credit institution has become aware in providing services or supporting any of its clients – whether an individual or a legal entity – represent a banking secret. Banks are subject to a stricter prohibition with respect to customer information. Unless there is a specific exemption under the Banking Law, banks are prohibited from sharing any customer confidential information with third parties without the customer's express instruction, even if an express consent was obtained in accordance with the GDPR.

[221] Generally, a bank is prohibited from providing information considered a banking secret without its customer's provable consent unless a specific exemption provided by the Credit Institutions Act stipulates otherwise. As there is neither a special regulation nor a specific exemption for disclosure of banking secrets in the scope of the due diligence process, measures must be adopted to ensure an adequate level of protection for the disclosed information.

15.3.5 Other Restrictions

[222] Disclosure restrictions similar to those relating to banking secrets apply to regulated companies such as: (i) insurance companies, where the insurance secrets of both individuals and corporate entities are protected pursuant to the Insurance Act; and (ii) investment firms, investment fund managers, venture capital fund managers, stock exchanges and clearing houses, pursuant to the Capital Markets Act.

[223] The Insurance Act provides instances in which the insurance company may disclose client information, including on the basis of the client's explicit consent. Nevertheless, even those instances do not relieve the insurance company of the obligation to ensure the protection of the disclosed information in the manner described above and in line with the personal data protection rules and regulations.

[224] The Capital Markets Act imposes a general duty of confidentiality on certain entities with respect to clients' personal data, which represent business secrets of such entities. There is an exemption from such confidentiality obligation when data must be disclosed to the competent regulatory agency, regulated market, administrative or judicial authorities, or when such disclosure is authorised by the client.

[225] In addition to this general non-disclosure obligation, the Capital Markets Act also contains a special regime for the protection of 'inside information'. Inside information is defined as information of a precise nature relating, directly or indirectly, to:

(a) a financial instrument, which is an investment instrument or other instrument, that has been admitted to trading on the Regulated Market or MTP, or for which admission to trading on the Regulated Market or MTP has been sought;
(b) a derivative financial instrument, which is an instrument that has not been admitted to trading on the Regulated Market and whose value derives from the value of a financial instrument;
(c) the issuer of a financial instrument; or
(d) any other fact having a significant effect on the quoted price or other price of a financial instrument or on its revenue.

Which is not public and which, if it were made public, could have a significant effect on the quoted price or revenue of the financial instrument or other instrument whose value is derived from the financial instrument.

Inside information is information of a precise nature if:

(a) it indicates a fact that exists or may reasonably be expected to come into existence in the future; and
(b) it is specific enough to enable a conclusion to be drawn as to the possible effect of such a fact on the price of the relevant financial instrument or other instruments derived from the financial instrument.

[226] Information which, if it were made public, could have a significant effect on the price or revenue of the financial instrument means information that a reasonable investor would be likely to use as part of the basis of its investment decisions.

[227] Should insider information be disclosed in the process of a due diligence review and be used to the benefit of and by the reviewer or any other third party, such insider information must, without undue delay, be made public by the target company.

[228] An issuer must also maintain a list of persons and/or entities who can access its inside information. The list is not published but should be provided to the Croatian Financial Services Supervisory Agency upon its request without undue delay.

16 ROLE OF THE COURTS

16.1 General

[229] The role of the courts in the Republic of Croatia is to protect legal order determined by the Constitution, the EU's acquis, international treaties and by the adopted laws, as well as to ensure uniform application of law. The independence of the judicial system is guaranteed by the Constitution of the Republic of Croatia. Nonetheless, the independence of Croatian courts has been called into question quite often in the past, especially in cases involving major social or political issues. Based on the European Commission's 2022 Rule of Law Report, (country chapter on the rule of law situation in Croatia), judicial independence is perceived as unsatisfactory – only 20% of the general population and 23% of companies perceived the level of independence of courts and judges to be 'fair or very good' in 2022. The Croatian judicial system is also inadequate in terms of the duration of court proceedings, and the capacity of the courts to deal with complex matters requiring specialized knowledge.

[230] In Croatia, disputes are generally resolved before the courts within civil proceedings. However, an increasing number of commercial disputes are resolved through arbitration, especially for complex disputes. Mediation is also available but rarely used.

[231] There are no apparent tendencies in Croatian court practice which would show different treatment for domestic residents and companies over those of foreigners, or favouring the rights of individuals over those of businesses. The only exception is in the area of labour law disputes, where courts tend to rule in favour of employees, where possible, which is strongly connected to the statutory regulation of the burden of proof, which in labour disputes lies with the employer.

[232] In terms of communication with Croatian courts, a pilot project launched in 2020 introduced a system of electronic communication (*Cro. e-komunikacija*) which allows for all written communication with the court to be carried out electronically. This mode of communication is mandatory for all legal entities incorporated in Croatia, which must seek access to the system from the Ministry of Justice and Administration, which access is granted in a simple, informal procedure.

16.2 Court System

[233] Croatia has a three-tiered judicial system, with courts of general and specialised jurisdiction. The first instance courts of general jurisdiction, dealing with civil and criminal cases, are composed of Municipal courts, while the County courts are the second instance courts of general jurisdiction, with some competences as for first instance courts. The courts of specialised jurisdiction comprise nine commercial and four administrative courts at first instance, and the High Criminal Court, the High Misdemeanour Court, the High Commercial Court and the High Administrative Court at second instance. The Supreme Court deals with all types of cases as the court of the highest instance. The Constitutional Court, as a fully separated judicial entity, rules on constitutional claims raised for the protection of violated rights and freedoms guaranteed by the Croatian Constitution and/or by the European Convention for Protection of Human Rights and Fundamental Freedoms, and on requests for assessment of constitutionality and legality of the laws and regulations.

[234] The structure, functions, and powers of the courts of both general and specialized jurisdiction are regulated by the Courts Act and by the Civil Procedure Act.

[235] The structure provided by the Acts in terms of courts' jurisdiction in civil and commercial matters is as follows:

(i) Municipal courts, as first-instance courts of general jurisdiction, decide in litigation, non-litigious and enforcement cases, labour disputes, inheritance and land register matters, procedures for recognition and enforcement of foreign courts' judgments and decisions, etc.
(ii) Commercial courts, as first-instance courts of specialised jurisdiction, decide in litigation cases between legal entities and/or natural persons in relation to performance of their registered activity, including disputes between shareholders, the company, members of the management and or supervisory board, in competition cases, disputes regarding IP and related rights, in liquidation and bankruptcy proceedings, court register matters, procedures of incorporation, operation and cessation of a company, procedures for recognition and enforcement of foreign courts' judgments and decisions, as well as of arbitration awards rendered in commercial disputes, etc.

(iii) County courts, as second instance courts of general jurisdiction, decide primarily on appeals against judgments and decisions of municipal courts.
(iv) The High Commercial court of the Republic of Croatia, as a second instance court of specialised jurisdiction, decides primarily on appeals against judgments and decisions of commercial courts. and
(v) The Supreme Court of the Republic of Croatia, as the court of highest instance, decides on extraordinary legal remedies against final judgments of Croatian courts, as well as on ordinary legal remedies when it acts as a second instance court, ensuring the uniform application of law and the equality of all in its application, and examines current issues of court practice.

[236] As a general rule, civil and commercial cases are decided at first instance by a single judge, while second instance courts, as well as the Supreme Court of the Republic of Croatia decide in a panel of three, and five judges in the case of the Supreme Court of the Republic of Croatia.

[237] Cases are assigned to an individual judge on the basis of an annual schedule by which court matters are allocated, which is set in advance at the end of each calendar year for the upcoming year. Cases are assigned to judges by algorithm on an automatic, random allocation basis.

16.3 Costs and Timing

[238] Costs connected to litigation usually include: (i) direct expenses incurred by parties in connection with court proceedings; (ii) court fees; (iii) the costs of obtaining evidence; (iv) experts' fees and the costs of translation and interpretation, as well as; (v) fees of attorney representation in court proceedings.

[239] The general rule is that each party will initially bear its own costs connected to litigation, incurred by its own actions. When deciding on the merits of the case, the court will rule by a decision which represents a part of the judgment, on the reimbursement of the costs borne by the parties, depending on who wins the claim. In practice, a party which is successful in litigation is generally awarded all costs reasonably incurred by it to successfully bring or defend against the raised claim. If a party is only partially successful, the court awards costs based on a calculation of the percentage of success of each party in the litigation. In any case, a party will have to reimburse the other party for those costs which have been incurred due to the former party's fault or accident. In relation to legal fees, however, compensation is awarded to a party according to a special tariff in accordance with rates set therein and irrespective of what the agreement between a party and its lawyer may be. The difference between the actual fees and awarded fees might thus be substantial.

[240] As for the court fees, their amount varies depending on the type of the proceeding being pursued. In litigation, a court fee is paid both for the claim and for the judgment – depending on the claim's value, but no more than HRK15 000.00 (approx. EUR1 990 00). For submission of legal remedies against the judgment (both ordinary and extraordinary), a court fee is paid depending on the claim's value as in the case of fees for claims and judgments, but with a 100% increase. If the fees for claims and/or appeals are paid either prior to, or simultaneously with the submission of a claim/appeal via an e-communication system, a party has the right to pay 50% of the determined amount of the fee. The same rule applies for the fees payable to court judgments delivered electronically, if such fee is paid within three days from delivery of the judgment.

[241] The main issue associated with pursuing a case before Croatian courts is the duration of court proceedings. Although the Civil Procedure Act imposes an obligation to finish the first-instance litigation proceeding within a reasonable timeframe, and certainly within three years from submission of the claim, according to a survey published by the European Commission in the 2022 Rule of Law Report, the average length of proceedings in the first instance courts in 2021 remained among the longest in the EU and mostly increased or stagnated, with as much as 1 000 days in litigious commercial cases. The average length of proceedings mostly decreased before the County courts, where litigious civil cases at second instance took, on average, 166 days. At first instance courts, backlogs decreased by 12% in commercial cases, but continued to increase by 22% in 2021 in litigious civil cases. Before the second instance High Commercial Court, the average length of proceedings decreased from 558 to 363 days, and so did the backlog (by about 25%).

[242] In cases of lengthy court proceedings, the Courts Act allows a party to seek protection of the right to trial within a reasonable time, by firstly requesting the relevant court to order a ruling judge to adopt a judgment (usually within six months), and subsequently to seek monetary compensation for incurred damages, which compensation can be awarded in the maximum amount of HRK35 000.00 (approx. EUR4 645.00).

16.4 Enforceability of Key Contractual Provisions

[243] It is not possible to generalise as to how easy or burdensome it is to enforce a key contractual provision in court, as this significantly depends on the attitude of the opposing party, the complexity of the factual aspects of the case and evidentiary procedure, as well as the punctuality and overall timeliness of the ruling judge. Also, certain contractual provisions might be easier to enforce than others. For example, restrictive covenants and confidentiality constraints might be decided quicker and more easily than warranty and indemnity claims, and indemnity claims might be decided quicker than warranty claims. Generally, whenever a claim for compensation or damages is brought to court, it may be expected that the litigation will last few years.

[244] The procedure required to enforce key contractual provisions may also depend on whether or not the SPA is executed in a form of a notarial deed, and whether it represents the enforcement title – enabling direct enforcement without the need to initiate litigation. Under Croatian law, a notarial deed may be directly enforceable if it unambiguously determines:

(i) the amount of the debtor's obligation; or
(ii) if it contains an express representation of the debtor by which it authorizes the creditor to initiate direct enforcement against the debtor without the debtor's further consent, upon the claim's maturity (an enforcement clause);
(iii) if it is signed in the form of a solemnized (notarial) deed.

[245] If the SPA contains all these elements, certain key contractual provisions could be enforced directly. However, it is unlikely that key contractual provisions would be enforced without ending up in litigation/arbitration first, even if the SPA contained all the above elements. The seller as enforcement debtor would most likely oppose the writ of enforcement upon which the court is obliged to refer the matter to litigation.

[246] In case of breach of key contractual provisions, a party whose right was breached, may: (i) commence a standard litigation; and/or (ii) file a motion for a preliminary injunction.

[247] A preliminary injunction is a kind of interim measure which may be granted by a court to secure an individual claim, whether before, during, or after the court proceeding, until the enforcement is effected. For a motion for preliminary injunction to be quickly dealt with, it must be demonstrated that there is an urgent need for such an interim measure. This condition is usually satisfied when it can be demonstrated that without such a measure, the claimant would be threatened by an objective danger of irreparable damage. This condition is also deemed to be satisfied when it can be demonstrated that without such measure, the opposing party would dispose or hide its assets in a way which would significantly endanger the settlement of the claim. In practice, the courts usually take a conservative approach when deciding on motions for preliminary injunctions and are far less inclined to issue preliminary injunctions unless they are absolutely convinced of the soundness of the proposal for issuing a preliminary injunction.

[248] Although the applicable Enforcement Act does not provide a timeframe in which the court must decide on a submitted motion for preliminary injunction, the Act envisages the principle of urgency in dealing with enforcement and preliminary injunction procedures.

[249] If the preliminary injunction is determined to be unfounded or unjustified on the part of the claimant, the claimant will be obliged to pay compensation to the opposing party for any damage suffered due to the existence of the preliminary injunction.

16.4.1 Restrictive Covenants

[250] If a contractual party fails to perform or breaches an obligation under the concluded agreement – for example, where the seller breaches the non-compete obligations – the purchaser may ask the court to order a preliminary injunction or can commence litigation against the seller, without requesting a preliminary injunction from the court.

[251] In such litigation, the damaged party may claim: (i) a ban on the other party competing with the business of the target; and/or (ii) damages; or (iii) payment of a contractual penalty, if so agreed in the SPA.

[252] The simplest way to proceed in such a case would be to claim a ban on the other party's recruitment of the sold company's key employees and the payment of the agreed contractual penalty.

[253] Under normal circumstances, it can be expected that the final judgment would be obtained within the average time that it takes for commercial disputes to be resolved, i.e., at least three years.

16.4.2 Confidentiality Constraints

[254] As in the case of a breach of restrictive covenants, if a party breaches the obligation of confidentiality under the concluded agreement, the other party may ask the court to order a preliminary injunction or can commence litigation without requesting the preliminary injunction.

[255] The injured party may claim: (i) a ban on the other party disclosing confidential information and/or (ii) damages or (iii) payment of a contractual penalty, if agreed in the SPA.

[256] The easiest way is to claim a ban on the other party disclosing confidential information and the payment of the agreed contractual penalty.

[257] Under normal circumstances, it may be expected that the final judgment would be obtained at around the average time for commercial disputes to be resolved, i.e., at least three years.

16.4.3 Protection of Minority Shareholder Rights

[258] Minority shareholders (shareholders holding shares with a nominal value of 5% or less of the registered share capital of a joint-stock company) are granted special protection under Croatian laws. For example, minority shareholders can: (i) request the board of directors to convene a general meeting and/or to put specific issues proposed by them on the general meeting's agenda (if the board of directors fails to do so, they may petition a court to authorise them to convene such a general meeting and/or amend the general meeting's agenda themselves, where the costs of such procedure are to be settled by the company); (ii) request the board of directors to include a proposed matter in the agenda of the general meeting; and (iii) prevent, i.e., object to settlement or waiver of any claim for compensation or damages by the company, as well as a general right of participation in general meetings, as well as notification and voting rights. Shareholders holding shares with a nominal value of at least 10% of the share capital are authorised to claim damages in the name of the company against members of the board of directors and members of the supervisory board who have breached their respective obligations resulting from the performance of their office.

[259] The law also provides minority shareholders with specific protection in the event of a squeeze-out. In the event of squeeze-out – which can be performed only in favour of the main shareholder holding shares in the nominal value of at least 95% of the company's share capital – minority shareholders have the right to adequate consideration in cash. The price of the consideration paid to the minority shareholders is determined by the main shareholder, which must consider the state of the company at the time of adoption of the general meeting's resolution. In order to convene a general meeting with an agenda to adopt such a resolution, the main shareholder must present to the management board a bank statement under which it jointly and severally guarantees payment of the determined amount of consideration, together with interest.

[260] A resolution of the general meeting on a squeeze out can be contested on grounds provided for in the Company Act, within thirty days of its adoption. Minority shareholders cannot contest the decision on squeeze out (unless the decision is otherwise void based on general grounds provided by the Company Act) but can request the court to determine the amount of adequate consideration for squeeze out. The court's determination as to the amount of adequate consideration is binding also in case of all other minority shareholders subject to the same squeeze out.

[261] Under normal circumstances, the average time for the obtaining of a final judgment would very likely be at least three years.

16.4.4 Enforcement of Warranty and Indemnity Claims

[262] If a contractual party breaches a warranty obligation, the recipient of the warranty may typically claim: (i) damages; and/or (ii) a reduction of the agreed purchase price; or (iii) payment of a contractual penalty if a contractual penalty was agreed upon under the SPA. Claims for damages and/or for reduction of the purchase price are associated with time-consuming litigation proceedings. This usually requires that the claimant obtains an expert valuation based on which the value of the claim in dispute will be ascertained before the litigation is initiated. Since the defendant would most likely oppose the valuation prepared by the claimant's experts, the court would appoint another expert (or several experts) to examine contentious valuations, which in turn significantly increases the costs of the dispute.

[263] The court fee for this type of claim would be determined based on the value of the claim.

[264] Under normal circumstances the average time for obtaining a final judgment in such a case would very likely be at least three years.

17 OTHER DISPUTE RESOLUTION MECHANISMS

17.1 Arbitration

[265] The most common dispute resolution mechanism for parties seeking to avoid litigation in court is arbitration. Arbitration is widely agreed upon in share purchase agreements as arbitrators are considered more prepared to handle complex cases. Arbitration is generally faster than normal court proceedings. In contrast to regular court proceedings, arbitration hearings are not open to the public, which sometimes makes it the preferred option. Arbitration decisions are recognized and enforced in the same way as ordinary court decisions. Arbitration decisions are not subject to appeal, but only to annulment that can be invoked only on limited grounds and within exact deadlines.

[266] For local deals, the parties would commonly agree in the SPA to refer their dispute to the Permanent Arbitration Court of the Croatian Chamber of Commerce (*Cro. Stalno arbitražno sudište pri Hrvatskoj gospodarskoj komori*).

[267] The Croatian Court of Arbitration is based in Zagreb. It has its own database of arbitrators (currently numbering 187 arbitrators for domestic arbitrations and arbitrations with a foreign element, and seventy-eight arbitrators with foreign residence, exclusively for arbitrations with a foreign element). Most of the arbitrators are legal professionals such as practicing attorneys, judges of Croatian high instance courts, as well as scholars.

[268] Proceedings are conducted under the Rules of Arbitration of the Permanent Arbitration Court (*Cro. Zagrebačka pravila*) unless the parties agree on the application of other rules of procedure.

[269] The administrative charges and registration fees, as well as the fees of the arbitrators depend on the value of the dispute, on the number or arbitrators and on the number of claimants and defendants. For example, the costs of arbitration before the Croatian Arbitration Court, with value of claim in dispute being EUR100 000, and which would be led by one arbitrator and involving one claimant and one defendant, would amount to approximately EUR5 847.64. In comparison with other arbitration centres, the Croatian Court of Arbitration is one of the less expensive ones.

17.2 Mediation

[270] Another form of alternative dispute resolution available in Croatia is mediation. Mediation can be performed either as in-court mediation or out-of-court mediation, with participation of one or more mediators. In the case of court mediation, mediators can only be judges of such court who have passed mediation training and are on the list of judge-mediators. In cases of out-of-court mediation, which are carried out before one of multiple centres or institutions for mediation, mediators have to possess special authorization and to be listed on the list of mediators. Additionally, mediation can be performed even outside of such out-of-court mediation centres and institutions, with only the participation of at least one mediator.

[271] Mediation is carried on with the participation of one or more mediators assisting the parties to find a mutually acceptable resolution to their dispute, but without any mandate to impose any sort of obligatory resolution on the parties.

[272] Mediation can be carried on irrespective of other court or arbitration proceedings being pursued with respect to the same dispute and/or matter, given that the main requirement for performance of mediation is willingness on both sides to achieve their dispute in this way and within this format.

[273] Successful mediation is concluded by a settlement agreed between the parties, which in the case of court mediation, can be also concluded in the form of a court settlement.

[274] Court mediation is free of charge for the parties, while the out-of-court mediation is charged based on the rates of the relevant mediation centre or institution engaged in the mediation process.

18 MERGER CONTROL/COMPETITION LAW ISSUES

18.1 General Introduction

[275] The core rules of Croatian competition law, including merger control, are laid down in the Croatian Act on Protection of Competition (Croatian official Gazette 79/2009, 80/2013, 41/2021, the 'Competition Act'). Croatian competition law is aligned with the EU competition law system. The authority in charge of surveying competition law is the Croatian Authority for the Protection of Economic Competition (the 'Competition Authority').

18.2 Merger Control Test

[276] A transaction must be notified to the Competition Authority if the following three conditions are satisfied:

(i) the transaction constitutes a concentration;
(ii) the turnover thresholds are met; and
(iii) the transaction is not subject to notification at the European Commission under Council Regulation No. 139/2004, on the control of concentrations between undertakings (the EU Merger Regulation (EUMR)).

[277] By way of exception, a transaction must also be notified to the Competition Authority, regardless of the turnover thresholds, if the transaction concerns the media market.

18.2.1 Concentration

[278] According to the Competition Act a concentration between undertakings arises with a change of control on a lasting basis:

(i) through merger of two or more independent undertakings or parts thereof;
(ii) by acquiring direct or indirect control or decisive influence by one or several undertakings over another or several other undertakings or part or parts of other undertakings:
- by acquiring the majority of stocks or shares; or
- by acquiring the majority of voting rights; or
- in another way in accordance with the provisions of the Companies Act.

[279] Acquisition of control may be achieved through the transfer of rights, contracts or by other means, by which one or more undertakings, either separately or jointly, taking into consideration all legal and factual circumstances, acquire the ability to exercise decisive influence over one or more other undertakings on a lasting basis.

[280] The creation of a joint venture by two or more independent undertakings performing on a lasting basis as an independent economic entity will also constitute a concentration.

[281] Two or more transactions within the meaning above that are implemented within a period of time of two years are regarded as a single concentration implemented on the day of the last transaction.

[282] In contrast, a concentration shall not be deemed to arise:

(i) when credit or other financial institutions, investment funds or insurance companies, in their regular business, (which includes trading and brokering of securities), whether for their own account or for the account of third parties, temporarily but for no longer than twelve months, acquire or hold stocks or shares with the intention of their further sale, and provided they do not use the right to vote with respect to that share or those shares in such a way as to affect the competitive behaviour of that undertaking. Upon request, the Agency can extend the period of twelve months if the undertaking proves that such a sale could not be carried out within the given period; or
(ii) the acquisition of shares or stocks as a result of internal restructuring of companies linked by common control (merger, transfer of ownership, etc.); or
(iii) when control over the undertaking has been transferred to a bankruptcy administrator or liquidator in accordance with the provisions of the Bankruptcy Act and the Companies Act or other applicable regulations.

18.2.2 Turnover Thresholds

[283] The second condition is satisfied if both of the following thresholds are met:

(i) the total annual consolidated income of all undertakings participating in the concentration, achieved through the sale of goods and/or services (hereinafter: total business income) on the world market, amounts to at least one billion HRK (approx. EUR132 m) in accordance with the financial reports for the financial year preceding the concentration, if at least one participant to the concentration has its seat and/or branch office in the Republic of Croatia; and

(ii) the total business income of each of at least two participants in the concentration, in the Republic of Croatia, according to the said financial statements, amounts to at least HRK100 000 000 (approx. EUR13 2 m) in the financial year preceding the concentration.

[284] The Competition Act also provides detailed rules for the calculation of turnovers.

18.2.3 Transaction Subject to European Merger Control

[285] Even though a transaction meets both the conditions stipulated above the transaction is not subject to notification at the Competition Authority if it is subject to notification at the European Commission under the EUMR. In such a case, the so-called one-stop shop principle applies, and the transaction is reviewed by the European Commission only.

18.3 Notification Procedure

[286] If all three conditions specified above are met or the transaction concerns the media market, the transaction is subject to notification at and the approval of the Competition Authority. This section addresses the issues concerning proceedings before the Competition Authority.

18.3.1 Notifying Party

[287] The undertaking(s) that is/are required to file a notification (and is/are responsible for failure to file a notification) is/are as follows:

Type of Concentration	*Notifying Undertaking(s)*
In case when one undertaking is acquiring control or decisive influence on the entire or part of undertaking	Undertaking acquiring the control

Type of Concentration	*Notifying Undertaking(s)*
In all other cases	All participants to the concentrations through one joint notification

18.3.2 Commencement of the Merger Proceedings

[288] The approval proceeding commences once the Competition Authority receives a completed standard notification or, where applicable, a simplified notification, of the concentration, including all the required documents. There is no specific deadline set for submission of the notification. The notification is to be submitted after the conclusion of the agreement by which the control or decisive influence is acquired or after the publication of the public offer by which the control or decisive influence is acquired. Exceptionally the notification can be submitted in advance if the parties in good faith prove the actual intention of concluding the agreement or if they publicly announce the intention to publish the public offer. However, until the transaction is approved by the Competition Authority, the concentrating undertakings are prohibited from implementing the transaction.

[289] The Competition Authority publishes the commencement of the proceedings on its website. In the announcement the Competition Authority also invites third parties to lodge their objections or opinions concerning the concentration.

18.3.3 Notification

[290] There are two possible forms of notification: (i) standard notification; and (ii) simplified notification. The latter can be used if the criteria listed by the Competition Act are met.

Standard Notification

[291] In a standard notification, the notifying undertakings must provide the Competition Authority with extensive information on the concentration. The documents and other information which must be provided to the Competition Authority are primarily set out in the Decree on the method of application and criteria for evaluating concentrations of undertakings of the Competition Authority (Croatian official Gazette 38/2011) (the 'Decree'). Pursuant to the Decree, the following documents must be submitted:

(i) the completed questionnaire for notification of the concentration;
(ii) powers of attorney (if the concentrating undertakings are represented in the proceedings by an attorney-at-law or by another proxy);
(iii) extracts of each of the concentrating undertakings from the Commercial Register or, if the undertakings are not Croatian entities, from any other similar register;
(iv) the undertakings' ownership and control structure charts;

(v) the document(s) establishing the concentration;
(vi) the undertakings' annual reports and audited financial statements for the last financial year;
(vii) the consolidated financial statements of the undertakings subject to the duty to prepare consolidated financial statements for the last financial year;
(viii) reports, analysis, studies and any other similar documents which have been prepared for any member of the Board of Directors or Supervisory Board (or of any other similar corporate body) or for the shareholders' meeting in order to assess the concentration.

[292] The documents must be in Croatian. If originals are not in Croatian, their translation must also be submitted. In practice, the Competition Authority does not require the translation of all documents if they are available in a commonly used foreign language (such as English).

[293] The core document concerning the notification is the questionnaire referred to in point (a).

Simplified Notification

[294] A simplified notification of a concentration may be filed in the event that:

(i) none of the concentrating undertakings operates within the same relevant product market and geographical market and there is no horizontal overlap between them or when none of the undertakings operates on a market that is ascending or descending with respect to the market on which the other undertaking operates so that there is no vertical connection between them; or
(ii) the concentrating undertakings operate in the same relevant product market and geographical market, but their combined share on such market is less than 20%, and at the same time, none of the undertakings operates on a product market that is ascending or descending with respect to the market on which the other undertaking operates, or their share in any such vertically connected market does not exceed 30% or more; or
(iii) an undertaking acquires sole control over a joint venture in which it has so far exercised joint control;
(iv) in cases where two or more undertakings acquire control of the joint venture, that does not have relevant activities in Republic of Croatia or when those relevant activities are not planned in reasonable time.

[295] Pursuant to the Decree, the notifying undertakings in the simplified notification procedure must provide the Competition Authority with a completed simplified questionnaire for the approval of the concentration and with the same documents as in the standard procedure, except for the reports analysis and studies.

18.3.4 Stages of the Proceedings

Standard Proceedings

Stages of Proceedings, Deadlines Referrals

[296] There are two possible stages regarding the proceedings. The first stage (commencing once the Competition Authority receives the complete notification) can take up to thirty days, whilst the second stage, if opened, can take up to an additional three months.

[297] If the Competition Authority fails to issue a decision within these periods of time, the transaction is deemed to be approved upon expiration of the periods. However, in both stages, the period may be suspended if the Competition Authority requests additional information on the concentration. Such requests automatically interrupt the proceedings and the above-mentioned periods of time do not continue to run until the information requested by the Competition Authority is provided.

Phase One

[298] At the beginning of the first phase, the Competition Authority assesses whether the transaction is subject to its approval. If the Competition Authority concludes that the transaction is not subject to its approval, it issues a decision to that effect and terminates the proceedings.

[299] If the transaction is subject to the Competition Authority's approval, the Competition Authority assesses whether the transaction is likely to significantly impede competition, particularly by creating or strengthening a dominant position of the concentrating undertakings.

[300] When assessing the impact of the transaction on competition, the Competition Authority assesses, in particular: (i) the structure of the relevant market, the existing and possible future competitors on the relevant market in the territory of Republic of Croatia or outside, the structure and choice of the offer and demand on the market and their trends, prices, risks, economical, legal and other obstacles to entering or exiting the market; (ii) the position, the market share and economic and financial strengths of the undertakings on the relevant market, the decree of competitiveness of the undertakings participants to the concentration, possible changes in the business activities of the participants to the concentration and alternative sources of supply for the purchasers that arise as consequence of the concentration; (iii) the effect of the concentration on other undertakings and consumers, as well as shorter distribution methods, reduction of transport costs or of distribution costs, specialization in production, technological innovation, reduction of the price of the products and/or services, as well as other advantages directly arising from the implementation of the concentration.

[301] Provided that the transaction does not significantly impede competition, the Competition Authority issues a decision approving the transaction.

[302] On the other hand, if the Competition Authority concludes that the transaction raises serious concerns of a significant impediment of competition, it notifies the notifying undertaking(s) of this fact and the proceedings enter into phase two.

Phase Two

[303] In the second phase, the Competition Authority investigates the market conditions and structure of competition in the relevant markets in greater detail, bearing in mind the need to preserve effective competition.

[304] If the Competition Authority concludes that the transaction would significantly impede competition, then it issues a decision by which it prohibits the transaction. On the other hand, if the Competition Authority concludes that the transaction does not significantly impede competition, then it issues a decision approving the transaction.

[305] The Competition Authority can also issue a decision by which the concentration is evaluated as approved conditional on the implementation of certain measures and deadlines specified by the Agency. This is the case when the Competition Authority during the evaluation proceeding ascertains that the concentration can be approved only with implementation of certain measure and deadlines. These measures and conditions can be proposed by the undertaking already in the notification of the concentration. If this has not been done, the Competition Authority will invite the undertaking to propose such measures and conditions within a one month period.

Simplified Proceedings

[306] When simplified notification is made, the Competition Authority either: (i) approves the concentration; or (ii) finds that it needs additional information to assess the concentration and issues a request that the party/parties to the proceedings submit a standard notification.

18.4 Implementation of the Transaction

18.4.1 Mandatory Suspension of Implementation

[307] Pursuant to the Competition Act, until the transaction is approved by the Competition Authority, the concentrating undertakings are prohibited from implementing the transaction.

18.4.2 Application for an Exemption

[308] The concentrating undertakings may apply to the Competition Authority, for an authorization to implement certain activities of the implementation of the transaction if there is a serious risk that they or other third entities will incur significant damage or any other serious detriment.

18.4.3 Consequences

[309] If the Competition Authority discovers that the concentrating undertakings have implemented the transaction without filing the notification or contrary to the decision by which the concentration is evaluated as prohibited, it is authorised, in addition to imposing the fines described below, to order the undertakings to 'sell or transfer', i.e., to sell the shares, transfer the business, prohibit or limit the exercise of voting rates related to the stocks of shares in undertaking, or order the termination of the joint venture or other means of achieving the control.

18.5 Competition Authority's Authorizations

18.5.1 Right to Information

[310] It is generally in the undertakings' interest to provide the Competition Authority with sufficient information on the transaction so that the proceedings can proceed smoothly and as quickly as possible.

[311] In addition, the Competition Authority is also authorized to request the undertakings to provide it with additional information. Failure to provide the Competition Authority with such information may lead to an interruption of the proceedings. The Competition Authority is also authorized to impose severe fines for failure to submit such information.

18.5.2 Power to Investigate

[312] The Competition Authority has extensive powers to investigate undertakings in the Republic of Croatia, e.g., to enter business premises and land, to examine business books or records and make copies or extracts, ask for explanations or seal off any business premises and books or records for the inspection period. Upon prior authorization by a court, the Competition Authority may even inspect private premises, including the homes of directors, managers, and other members of staff of the respective undertakings.

18.6 Fines and Remedial Measures

18.6.1 Fines

[313] The Competition Authority may impose severe fines for breaching merger control regulations. These fines may amount up to:

(i) 10% of the total worldwide income that the undertaking achieved in the last financial year in the event of implementation of a prohibited concentration that can significantly affect competition, especially if it is a consequence of strengthening the existing or creating a new dominant position of the participants to the concentration;

(ii) 1% of the total income achieved in the last financial period for failing to submit information requested by the Competition Authority, for submission of incorrect, incomplete, or false information in the notification, or for implementing the concentration without effecting the measures approved by the Competition Authority or contrary to the decision of the Competition Authority.

18.6.2 Remedial Measures

[314] The Competition Authority may, in addition to the above fines, impose remedial measures to be taken by the undertakings and may set reasonable deadlines for their implementation. The Competition Authority may, e.g., order the undertakings to 'sell or transfer' or to adopt other measures listed above.

19 TAXATION ASPECTS

19.1 Nature of the Tax Regime

[315] The Croatian tax system can be described as pluralistic, which means that there are several layers of taxation:

(i) state taxes;
(ii) county taxes;
(iii) municipal taxes;
(iv) common taxes.

On top of taxes proper (*porezi*), there are a number of other public dues that tax authorities assess, collect or enforce, such as customs duties, public fees, contributions or concession fees.

Main taxes include:

(i) Personal income tax.
(ii) Value added tax.
(iii) Corporate income tax.
(iv) Excise taxes.

19.2 Liability to Tax

[316] Corporate income tax (literally: 'profit tax') payers comprise:

(i) a company or another legal or natural person resident of the Republic of Croatia, which performs its economic activity independently, permanently, and with a view to achieving profits, income, or revenue, or other business relevant benefits;

(ii) a domestic permanent establishment of a foreign entrepreneur (non-resident);

(iii) self-employed natural persons if he or she declares that they will pay corporate income instead of personal income tax;

(iv) self-employed natural persons generating a total income greater than EUR995.421 06 in the previous tax period;

(v) all entrepreneurs or their legal successors which are not defined as taxpayers elsewhere, but who are not personal income taxpayers under the regulations on personal income taxation and whose profit is not taxed elsewhere.

[317] Taxpayers may be both Croatian tax residents and tax non-residents. Croatian tax residents are legal and natural persons whose registered office is registered in the commercial or other registry or record in the Republic of Croatia, or whose place of effective management and supervision is in the Republic of Croatia. Residents are also entrepreneurs – natural persons with permanent residence or habitual residence in the Republic of Croatia, whose activity is inscribed in a registry or record.

[318] Residents are taxed based on profit generated domestically and abroad. Non-residents are taxed on profit generated domestically, subject to the provisions of applicable double taxation treaties. Croatia is party to sixty-six (as of 30 December 2022) double taxation treaties.

19.2.1 Corporate Tax Rate

[319] Corporate income tax rate for 2022 was:

- 10% if, during the taxation period, revenue has been generated up to HRK7 500 000.00 (EUR995.421 06); or
- 18% if, during the taxation period, revenue has been generated greater than HRK7 500 000 (EUR995.421 06).

[320] The tax base is the profit that is assessed pursuant to accounting regulations as the difference between revenue and expenditures before the profit tax calculation, but increased or reduced pursuant to the provisions of this Act.

19.2.2 Taxes on Capital Gains

[321] Capital gains of a Croatian corporate resident are taxed in accordance with general rules on corporate income tax, i.e., they are included in the corporate income tax base.

[322] Capital gains of a Croatian personal income taxpayer are in general calculated on a 10% basis.

[323] Profit on the sale of shares/an ownership interest is calculated on the basis of the difference between the purchase and sale price (or market price).

19.2.3 CFC Rules

[324] Rules for the taxation of controlled foreign companies (CFC) have been implemented into Croatian tax law according to the EU Anti-Avoidance Directive (ATAD). Selected income of a foreign controlled company (such as income from dividends, interest, and royalties) will form part of the tax base of the Croatian controlling company that holds directly or indirectly more than 50% of the share of the controlled company, or that participates in more than half of its profit or voting rights. The rule is subject to several exceptions, e.g., it will not be applied if the foreign company carries out substantial business activity and if income that would be subject to the tax base of the Croatian controlling company constitutes less than one-third of the controlled company.

19.2.4 Value Added Tax or Sales Taxes or Other Taxes on Revenue/Sales

[325] Value Added Tax (VAT) law has been harmonized with the relevant EU Directives.

[326] The standard VAT rate is 25%, the first reduced VAT rate is 13% and the second reduced VAT rate is 5%.

[327] A taxpayer is:

(i) Any person who independently performs any economic activity regardless of the purpose or result of performing that activity.
(ii) Any person who occasionally supplies new means of transport (e.g., citizens and ministries).
(iii) A taxpayer who does not have headquarters, a permanent establishment or a permanent or habitual residence in the territory of the Republic of Croatia and who carries out a supply of goods or services on the home territory which is taxable in the Republic of Croatia (unless VAT is paid by the goods or services recipient from Croatia). Taxpayers who have headquarters in the European Union may appoint a tax representative in the Republic of Croatia, while taxpayers with headquarters outside the European Union have to appoint a tax representative as the person liable to pay VAT.
(iv) State government bodies, state administration bodies, the bodies and units of local and regional self-government, chambers and other bodies governed by public law if performing economic or other activity, and non-taxation of those activities would result in a distortion of market competition.

[328] A legal person with headquarters, a permanent establishment, or a natural person with permanent or habitual residence in Croatia, whose value of goods supplied or services performed in the previous or current calendar year did not exceed HRK300 000 (EUR39.816 84) shall be exempted from VAT.

19.2.5 Stamp Duties or Other Taxes on Land Transactions

[329] Real estate transfer tax is paid at the 3% rate. If VAT is paid for the real estate transaction, real estate transfer tax does not apply.

[330] Contribution of real property into the share capital of a company, or if real estate is transferred as a consequence of corporate merger, does not trigger real estate transfer tax.

19.2.6 Other Taxes on Land or Real Estate

[331] While the authorities tease the introduction of real estate tax for some time now, such tax has not been introduced yet.

[332] There are some other public dues that are related to real estate such as water management contributions or utility fees. The owner or user of property pays a 'utility fee' (*komunalna naknada*) for the following:

(i) residential area;
(ii) garage space;
(iii) business premises;
(iv) construction land used for business activities;
(v) undeveloped construction land.

19.2.7 Capital Duties or Other Duties on Share Capital

[333] No capital duty is levied on share capital.

19.2.8 Business Rates

[334] No special business rates are levied in Croatia.

19.2.9 Taxes Imposed on Employers (For Example, PAYE and Social Security Obligations)

[335] When paying out salaries, employers withhold and pay on behalf of the employee several taxes and other public dues:

(i) social security contributions of 15% (state pension scheme) and 5% (pension funds);
(ii) personal income tax – 20% or 30%, depending on the income;
(iii) municipal income tax – rate depending on the municipality in question;
(iv) health insurance contribution – 16.5%.

19.2.10 Customs and Excise Duties

[336] Custom duties can be levied on imports from countries outside the EU. Excise duty is levied on alcohol and alcoholic beverages, tobacco products, energy products and electricity. Rates of excise duty differ according to the kind of goods.

19.2.11 R&D Costs

[337] R&D is incentivised by way of tax incentives. Companies can claim tax relief for research and development projects that belong to the categories of fundamental research, industrial research, experimental development, or for feasibility studies. The support is realized as a right to an additional reduction of the base of profit tax or income tax for justified expenses.

19.2.12 Exit tax

[338] Tax legislation does not provide for any exit tax in case of relocation of the company from Croatia to another country.

19.3 Tax Consolidation. Group Relief of Gains and Losses

[339] A tax loss is transferred and compensated by reducing the tax base during the next 5 years, unless otherwise provided by the law. In reducing the tax base for losses from previous taxation periods, the tax base is first reduced by older losses.

19.4 Tax Considerations Arising on M&A Transactions

[340] A natural person – being a resident who is a holder of financial assets, is under obligation to calculate, suspend and pay tax on income from capital based on capital gains, except for capital gains based on the alienation of shares in the capital of a trading company that are not transferable on the capital market in accordance with a special regulation, by the last day of the month of February of the current year for all capital gains realized in the previous year, as reduced by any realized capital losses at a rate of 10%.

[341] Profit on a sale realised by a Croatian corporate resident is included in the annual corporate income tax return

[342] Profit on the sale of shares/an ownership interest in a Croatian company realised by a non-Croatian tax resident is generally not taxable in Croatia.

[343] The acquisition price of shares is tax-deductible for the buyer upon the disposal of the shares. No 'step-up' can be achieved in the tax base of the underlying assets owned by the target, since the transfer does not affect the acquisition costs.

[344] Withholding tax is applied to profit generated by a non-resident of the Republic of Croatia. It is paid in respect of interest, dividends, profit shares, royalties and other intellectual property rights (including reproduction rights, patents, licences, copyrighted marks, designs, or models, manufacturing procedures, production formulas, sketches, plans, industrial or scientific experience, and other similar rights) paid to foreign persons that are not natural persons.

19.4.1 Transfer Taxes

[345] The transfer of shares is not subject to VAT, real estate transfer tax or any other taxes or stamp duties.

19.4.2 Transfer of Tax Liabilities

[346] The buyer 'inherits' the tax history of the acquired company, including its latent tax liabilities. Some buyers use deferred payments or retentions, but it is generally impracticable for non-identified risks given the lengthy statute of limitations for potential tax avoidance issues.

[347] The right and obligation of the tax authorities to determine tax liability and interest, the right and obligation to initiate the process of collection of taxes, interest and enforcement expenses and the right of the taxpayer to a tax refund or refund of interest and enforcement expenses expires after six years from the date when the statute of limitations began to run:

(1) The statute of limitation on the right to assessment of tax liabilities and interest begins to run after the year in which tax liabilities and interests should have been assessed.
(2) In case of tax fraud or similar offences, the right to assessment of tax liabilities and interest commences after the year in which the final judgment for a criminal offence has been passed.
(3) The statute of limitations on the collection of tax, interest and enforcement expenses starts running after the year in which the taxpayer self-assessed the tax liability or after the year in which the decision based on which the tax authority established the tax base and interest became executable, or after the year in which the tax liability became due.
(4) The statute of limitations on tax refund, interest and enforcement expenses starts running after the year in which the taxpayer acquired the right to a refund.

19.4.3 Real Estate Transfer Tax

[348] The transfer of real estate is subject to a real estate transfer tax (please *see* above) unless it is subject to VAT, or in case of other statutory exemptions.

19.4.4 VAT

[349] The transfer of movable assets and, in certain cases, real property is subject to VAT.

[350] VAT is payable on:

(i) the delivery of a building (or its part) that has never been occupied or used, including the land on which it is located;
(ii) the delivery of a building (or its part), including the land on which it is located, where no more than two years have passed from the date of first occupancy or use until the date of the next delivery;
(iii) delivery of construction land.

[351] No VAT is payable on the delivery of a building or part of it, including the land on which it stands:

(i) if the same building (or part of it) was occupied or used;
(ii) if more than two years have passed from the date of first occupancy or use of the building to the date of the next delivery of the building.

A taxable person entered into the registry of VAT taxable persons in the Republic of Croatia must pay VAT on the purchase of real property, but this is otherwise non-VAT-taxable if the seller opted for VAT taxation.

19.4.5 Transfer of Tax Liabilities

Sale of Assets

[352] If an enterprise is the subject matter of a transaction by way of an asset deal, liability may be partially transferred to the acquirer. The acquirer is considered a tax guarantor for:

(1) tax payable based on the business activities of the economic entity before acquisition;
(2) withholding tax (tax on income from employment) on the condition that the tax obligation was created in the year in which the transfer of ownership of the economic entity was performed.

[353] The guarantee of the acquirer is limited to the value of the acquired assets.

Merger

[354] In the case of a merger or division, the taxpayers shall be obliged to include the previously declared value adjustments or valuation of assets into the tax. If such a taxpayer has no declared adjustments and was not obliged to execute, did not execute, and should not execute specific value adjustments under an accounting regulation, then the actions bear no effect on taxation.

[355] If the transfer of the right for compensation of losses takes place within the context of mergers or divisions to legal successors during the taxation period, the right to loss transfer starts in the period in which the legal successor acquired the right to loss transfer.

19.5 Structuring the Investment: Withholding Taxes

19.5.1 Dividends Paid to Foreign Corporate/Group Shareholders

[356] The distribution of profits/dividends is subject to withholding tax levied at a rate of 10%. Withholding tax can be reduced or eliminated based on double taxation treaties.

[357] Withholding tax for dividends is not paid when the dividends are paid to a company that has one of the forms for which the common taxation system is applied, valid for parent companies and associated companies from different EU Member States, if:

(1) the recipient of the dividend or profit share has at least 10% of the capital of the company paying the dividend or profit share;
(2) if the lowest percentage is held without interruption for twenty-four months.

19.5.2 Dividends Paid to Foreign Individual Shareholders

[358] The distribution of profits/dividends is subject to withholding tax levied at a rate of 10%. Withholding tax can be reduced or eliminated on the basis of double taxation treaties.

19.5.3 Dividends Received from Foreign Subsidiaries/Affiliates

[359] Dividends from foreign subsidiaries may reduce the corporate income tax base. The tax base is reduced for dividends where:

(a) the payer is a profit taxpayer pursuant to this Act, or a payer of an equivalent tax type; and
(b) the payer is an organization with a legal form comparable to a limited liability company, company or other person whose legal form and accounting and taxation method is comparable to profit taxpayers pursuant to this Act; and
(c) that are not a tax-deductible expenditure or deductible for the payer.

[360] When a dividend is generated from EU Member States, the conditions for reduction are met if the payer is:

(a) a payer of one of the taxes for which the common taxation system is applied, valid for parent companies and associated companies in different EU Member States, pursuant to the list in the Annex which is an integral part of the Profit Tax Ordinance adopted by the Minister of Finance; and
(b) a company having one of the forms for which the common taxation system is applied, valid for parent companies and associated companies in different EU Member States, pursuant to the list in the Annex which is an integral part of the Profit Tax Ordinance adopted by the Minister of Finance; and
(c) a resident of a EU Member State pursuant to the law in that State, and is not applied to non-residents outside of the EU, pursuant to international agreements for the avoidance of double taxation, concluded with non-Member States.

19.5.4 Interest Paid to Foreign Corporate/Group Shareholders or Affiliates

[361] Interest paid to a non-Croatian tax resident is generally subject to a 15% withholding tax unless provided for otherwise in a double taxation treaty. Furthermore, the withholding tax on interest charged between related entities can generally be eliminated under the conditions set out in the EU Interest-Royalties Directive.

[362] Statutory exemption from withholding tax on interest are as follows:

(1) for merchandise loans for the procurement of goods used for the performance of business activity of the taxpayer;
(2) for loans given by a foreign bank or other financial institution;
(3) to possessors of bonds, both state and corporate, that are foreign legal persons.

19.5.5 Interest Received from Foreign Corporate/Group Shareholders or Affiliates

[363] Such income is subject to general corporate income tax. In determining interest revenue from loans given between affiliated parties, interest is calculated on the basis of the amount of the interest rate that would have been realised between non-affiliated parties at the time of loan approval. In determining interest expenditure from loans received between affiliated parties, interest is recognized at most to the amount of the interest rate that would have been realised between non-associated parties at the time of loan approval.

19.5.6 Intellectual Property (IP) Royalties Paid to Foreign Corporate/Group Shareholders or Affiliates

[364] Royalties paid to a non-Croatian tax resident are generally subject to 15% withholding tax unless provided for otherwise in a double taxation treaty. Furthermore, the withholding tax on interest charged between related entities can generally be eliminated under the conditions set out in the EU Interest-Royalties Directive.

19.5.7 Intellectual Property (IP) Royalties Received from Foreign Corporate/Group Shareholders or Affiliates

[365] Such income is subject to general corporate income tax.

19.5.8 Management or Consultancy Fees Paid to Foreign Corporate/Group Shareholders or Affiliates

[366] Fees for management or consultancy services performed in the territory of Croatia and paid to corporate/group shareholders within the European Union are either not liable to withholding tax or give rise to the creation of a Croatian permanent establishment.

19.5.9 Payments to Non-residents in Respect of the Purchase or Renting of Immovable Property

[367] Domestic and foreign natural or legal persons are equated with regard to the payment of real estate transfer tax unless otherwise specified in an international agreement.

[368] Taxes on lease payments vary greatly on the status of the parties involved, their income and the purpose of the immovable property. Lessors and lessees of real property may be liable for property income tax, income tax surcharge, profit tax, value added tax, lump sum tourist tax, holiday house tax or prescribed contributions.

19.5.10 Double Tax Treaties

[369] Croatia is party to 66 (as at 30 December 2021) double taxation treaties. The Croatian model, based on the Organization for Economic Co-operation and Development (OECD) model, is used as the starting point during the negotiations, however, the provisions of individual treaties may differ.

19.6 Debt Financing

19.6.1 Are Finance Costs Associated with the Acquisition Generally Deductible

[370] In the case of an asset deal, the interest on acquisition financing is generally tax-deductible.

19.6.2 Deductibility of Exceeding Borrowing Costs

[371] A taxpayer may establish the excess borrowing costs incurred in a tax period as tax deductible expenditure only up to:

(1) 30 % of earnings before interest, taxes, depreciation, and amortization (EBITDA) or
(2) EUR3.000.000 00 if a greater amount is thus achieved.

19.7 Thin Capitalization

[372] Thin capitalization rules apply in Croatia and may limit the tax deductibility of interest payments and other related financial costs related to debt financing from related parties.

[373] Non-deductible interest includes interest for loans accepted from shareholders holding at least 25% of share capital or voting rights in relation to that amount of the loan which exceeds four times the amount of the shareholder's share in the capital or their voting power (unless the lender is a financial organization). Shareholder loans include third-party loans guaranteed by the shareholder or loans from related parties.

19.8 Transfer Pricing

[374] Prices between related parties must be set at fair market value for tax purposes. 'Related parties' include parties where one party participates directly or indirectly in the management, supervision, or capital of the other party, or both parties participate directly or indirectly in the management, supervision or capital of the company.

[375] Business dealings between related parties will be recognized only if the taxpayer possesses and, at the demand of the tax administration, provides data and information on related parties and business dealings with those parties, as well as methods used for determining comparable market prices and reasons for choosing those specific methods as well as the adjustment method.

20 EMPLOYMENT CONSIDERATIONS

20.1 General Introduction

[376] Employment in Croatia is regulated primarily by the Labour Act (Official Gazette Nos 93/2014–151/22) the 'Labour Act'), the Occupational Health and Safety Act (Official Gazette Nos 71/2014, 96/2018) and the Act on Representativeness of Employers´ Associations and Trade Unions (Official Gazette Nos 93/2014, 26/21).

20.2 Employment Contracts

20.2.1 General Concept

[377] Croatian labour law is oriented to the protection of employees. Croatian courts and administrative bodies generally apply labour law in a way more favourable to the employee, following the *in favorem laboris* principle.

[378] Most provisions in the Labour Act are mandatory; however, parties to employment contracts may deviate from the Labour Act by stipulating terms which are more favourable to the employee than conditions set out in the law. Employer, employer associations and unions may deviate by stipulating less favourable terms only if such deviation is explicitly provided by law.

20.2.2 Obligatory Contents

[379] A valid employment contract must contain at least the following:

(i) information on the parties;
(ii) the place where the work will be performed, or if it will be performed in various places;
(iii) the designation or type of work in which the employee will be engaged or a brief description of work;
(iv) the date on which the employee starts work;
(v) the date of the contract and the date on which the employee starts work;
(vi) whether the contract is entered for unlimited or fixed term, and duration of contract, if it is a fixed term contract;
(vii) duration of paid annual leave, or method of determination;
(viii) termination terms;
(ix) essential salary, increased salary, and periods of its payment;
(x) duration of working day or week, and whether full time or part time;
(xi) employees right to education, training and professional development, if contracted;
(xii) trial period terms, if it is contracted.

[380] An employment contract must be concluded in writing, or the employer must issue a written confirmation which shall include all of the above proscribed content. Even though a lack of written form does not render an employment contract invalid, an employer may be penalised by the relevant Work Inspectorate for a breach of its obligation to issue a confirmation of concluded employment contract with a fine up to EUR13.270 00, and up to EUR1 320 for responsible person of the employer. The Work Inspectorate is a part of the State Inspectorate and supervises the fulfilment of the obligations arising from the labour law regulations.

[381] In addition to the above, parties to an employment contract may agree on other conditions (e.g., that the employee be required to undertake business travel, that the employee not engage in competition with the employer after termination of the employment contract).

[382] Employment may be part-time or full-time and may be entered into for a fixed or an unlimited term. Employment is presumed to be entered into for an unlimited term unless the contract provides for a specific term.

Trial period

[383] An employment contract may provide for a trial period lasting six months unless a shorter period has been agreed upon. The trial period must be agreed upon in writing to be valid, and it may not be extended, unless the employee was temporarily absent from work during the trial period, especially due to temporary inability to work, use of maternity and parental rights according to a special regulation and use of the right to paid leave. The employment contract can be terminated where the employee shows unsatisfactory results during the trial period. Minimum notice period is seven days.

Pensions

[384] The pension system of Croatia is based on a three-pillar pension scheme. The first two pillars are mandatory, and employers and employees contribute. The third pillar is voluntary and is based on individual payments of employees, while employers can also contribute to private pension funds.

20.3 Non-competition

20.3.1 Non-competition During Employment

[385] During employment, an employee may engage in gainful activity identical to the employer's scope of business only with the employer's prior written consent. The employer may revoke such consent in writing at any time. If the employee breaches this obligation, the employer can claim damages or require that the profits from the competitive business are turned over to the employer. If the employer knew, at the time of concluding the employment agreement, that the employee performed certain business within the scope of business activity of the employer and did not request the employee to cease such activity, it is deemed that the employer granted permission to perform such activities.

20.3.2 Non-competition after Termination of Employment

[386] Parties to an employment contract may agree on a non-competition agreement, under which the employee undertakes not to accept the employment with another person which is in market competition with the employer, and/or not to engage in any activities which would compete with the employer's business activities, for a period of up to two years following the termination of the employee's employment.

The employer must undertake to provide the employee with compensation in the minimum amount of one half of the employee's average monthly salary (in the last three months before termination of employment agreement) for each month of compliance with the non-competition obligations. The non-competition arrangement may be set out in a separate agreement, but more often it is a clause within the employment contract. It must be made in writing and must comply with the above conditions, otherwise it is invalid. The employer can withdraw from the non-competition agreement (or clause) only before the end of the relevant employment, provided that such entitlement to withdraw is stipulated in the law or in the agreement between the parties (including relevant reasons for such withdrawal).

[387] Parties may also agree on the contractual penalty for breach of the non-compete agreement by the employee. In case that at the time of entering into the non-compete agreement the employee was receiving the salary that is higher than the average salary in the Republic of Croatia, the contractual penalty can be agreed even in cases where the employer did not assume the obligation to pay the compensation to the employee for the duration of the non-compete agreement.

20.4 Fixed-term Employment Contracts

20.4.1 Restrictions

[388] The Labour Code contains restrictions on employers regarding the conclusion of an employment contract for a fixed term.

The fixed-term employment between the parties can be entered into for a maximum of three years in total. That is, if the first fixed-term employment is concluded for one year, it may be subsequently extended for a maximum of an additional two years. After expiry of the three-year period, the employer wishing to extend the employment relationship is obliged to offer the employee an employment contract for indefinite period.

The Labour Act sets out exceptions to the above-mentioned restriction in duration of fixed term contract where it is possible to extend the duration of fixed term contract over three-year period. The first exception applies whenever it is provided in specific regulations or in a collective agreement for objective reasons. The second exception applies if a fixed-term contract is necessary for replacement of a temporarily absent employee, and the third exception applies if extension of a fixed term contract is necessary for the completion of work on a project that includes financing from EU funds.

20.4.2 Consequences

[389] The Employer is obliged to secure identical working conditions for employees with fixed-term contract and those with indefinite period contracts, i.e., there must be no differentiation in the rights and treatment of fixed-term employees.

20.5 Employment of Top-level Managers

[390] The Croatian Labour Act does not distinguish between the employment of 'ordinary employees' and managers in 'lower positions' and employment of 'top-level managers'. All of these categories are employed under the employment agreement, with the main difference being that the employment agreements of top-level managers usually include specific clauses on bonuses and other rights. Board members (directors) are not obliged to be employed by the company, so their status is usually regulated by specific managerial agreements.

20.5.1 Defining a Top-Level Manager

[391] There is no definition of a Top-Level Manager under the Labour Act.

20.5.2 Dismissal or Resignation of Top-Level Managers

[392] Since top-level managers are considered to be regular employees, no special rules regarding the termination of their office apply. If top-level managers are also appointed board members, they must be revoked from their position by shareholders resolution or they must offer their resignation. However, such recall or resignation only terminates a top-level manager's office as a top-level manager and has no effect on his/her employment with the company, unless it is specifically agreed in the employment contract that a termination of office will represent a special reason for termination of employment contract.

[393] The requirement for the recall or resignation to be valid is that it must be in writing and delivered to the other party.

20.6 Termination of the Employment Contract

[394] Employment may be terminated by agreement, by notice, by immediate cancellation or by court decision. Fixed-term employment also ends with the expiry of the period for which the employment was agreed (i.e., a fixed-term employment could also be terminated by any of the means stipulated below).

20.6.1 Termination by Agreement

[395] Employment may be terminated by agreement at any time and for any reason. The agreement must be in writing. The agreement must be in written form, but the Labour Act does not provide for any mandatory contents of such agreement, so the parties may freely dispose of their rights and obligations arising out of the employment relationship.

20.6.2 Termination by Notice

[396] Employment may be terminated by notice given by either the employer or the employee. The notice must be in writing and delivered to the other party; otherwise, it is without legal effect. Whereas the employer may only serve notice on the employee for certain reasons prescribed by the Labour Act and the notice must clearly set out the reason for the termination, the employee may serve notice at will without stating any reason for termination.

[397] Where the employer terminates the employment agreement by notice, the minimum notice period depends on the duration of the employment. The following statutory minimums are prescribed by the Labour Act:

Notice Period	*Duration of Continuous Employment*
2 weeks	<1 year
1 month	1 year
1 month 2 weeks	2 years
2 months	5 years
2 months 2 weeks	10 years
3 months	20 years
3 months 2 weeks	20 years, if employee age over 50
4 months	20 years, if employee age over 55

In cases where the employee terminates the employment agreement by notice for an important reason (e.g., a new job opportunity) the maximum notice period is one month. The employer and the employee may agree on a longer notice period, however, such notice period must be the same for both parties and according to jurisprudence, must not be to the detriment of the employee.

[398] The notice period runs from the delivery of the termination notice. If the employee serves notice for reasons connected to the transfer of his employment relationship, the employment terminates no later than on the day preceding such transfer.

(i) The employer may serve notice on the employee only for the following reasons, which must exist at the time when notice is given – otherwise the notice is invalid:
   (a) the employee becomes redundant as a result of economic, technological or organization reasons (business redundancy);
   (b) if the employee is unable to regularly perform his work duties because of his personal characteristics (personal reasons);
   (c) if the employee breaches his or her obligations arising out of the employment relationship (fault of employee);
   (d) if the employee does not perform satisfactorily within the trial period.

(ii) The reason under paragraph **[398] (iii) (a)** above includes situations where the employer conducts changes in his organization structure and as a consequence, the employee becomes redundant. In that case the employer may not hire a new employee in the same position for at least six months.

(iii) The reason under paragraph **[398] (iii) (b)** deals with the case in which an employee no longer meets the prerequisites for the performance of the agreed work. This reason may be applied, for example:
   (a) if the employee does not meet the legal requirements for the performance of the agreed work (e.g., a professional driver has a driver's licence that has been suspended);
   (b) if the employee does not meet the standards of performance set by the employer, without this being the fault of the employer; or
   (c) if the employee's work performance is unsatisfactory.

(vi) The reason in paragraph **[398] (iii) (c)** concerns an employee's violation of working discipline. In order for the employer to terminate employment, the violation must be caused by the employee – that is to say, the employee has to engage in wilful or negligent behaviour. The employee must have committed a serious violation of working discipline (e.g., drinking alcohol at work). Notice may be given for a less serious violation (e.g., late arrival for work) which has reoccurred if, during the last six months, the employee has been warned in writing of the possibility of his/her being dismissed in connection with said violation of working discipline. A reoccurring violation is usually interpreted to mean a violation that occurs a total of three times.

(iv) The employer may dismiss the employee due to misconduct only within a period of two months from the day on which it learned of the grounds for such dismissal, but no later than one year after the day on which those grounds arose.

(v) Employers should be cautious when using the termination reason set out in paragraph **[398] (iii) (c)** as the case law interpreting it is still limited and usually goes in favour of employee. What is meant by a gross breach of employment relationship obligations is interpreted on a case-by-case basis and while case law may provide certain guidelines, it should be interpreted on a non-reliance basis.

(vi) The law provides a protection period during which the employer may not serve notice on the employee. This protection applies to employees who are pregnant, on parental leave, on sickness leave, who permanently care for a child with increased needs, or a child with development impairments. In case of redundancy reasons applicable to such employees, the employer is obliged to ensure the return to the same position as before. In case such position has become redundant, the employer is obliged to ensure an equivalent position. Certain limitations on the service of notice also apply to workers who are on military or civil service or night workers who are temporarily unable to perform night work.

20.6.3 Immediate Cancellation

[399] Both employer and employee may cancel employment summarily/immediately, without notice, only in exceptional cases, for a severe breach of employment relationship or because of some other important circumstance where continuance of employment is no longer possible. The immediate cancellation must be given within a period of fifteen days from the date on which the employer/employee discovered the fact on which the immediate cancellation is based.

20.6.4 Collective Dismissal

[400] Collective dismissal is the termination of the employment of more than twenty employees within a nintety-day period, where at least five of those employees would have to be terminated for grounds under paragraph **[398] (iii) (a)**. This quota also includes the employees who agree to terminate the employment by agreement.

At least thirty days before giving notice to individual employees, the employer is required to inform the competent trade union body or employee council of its intention. At the same time, the employer is required to enter negotiations with the employee council on measures to avoid the collective dismissal or mitigate the negative consequences thereof for the employees, and in particular on the possibility of their employment in other suitable positions with the employer. Even though the objective of such negotiations is to reach an agreement between the employer and the trade union body or employee council, failure to reach any such agreement does not prevent any collective dismissal. The employer is obliged to consult with the employee council to achieve agreement regarding the necessity to reduce number of employees.

The employer is further required to inform a competent Employment Office in writing on the outcome of negotiations with the trade union body or employee council. In the report, the employer must specify the total number of its employees and the number of employees and positions to which the collective dismissal applies. If the employer does not fulfil this obligation towards the Employment Office, the collective dismissal is ineffective. It will remain ineffective until expiry of at least thirty days after the delivery by the employer of its report to the Employment Office.

20.6.5 Participation of Employee Council or Trade Unions in Termination of Employment

[401] An employer wishing to dismiss an employee by notice or by immediate cancellation is obliged to consult with the worker council, if one is established, or with a trade union representative active with the employer and which has the rights and obligations of the employee council.

If the employer wishes to dismiss a worker council member or a trade union representative, then the employer must seek the prior consent of the employee council or trade union to such dismissal. Consent is also considered to have been given if the competent trade union body does not refuse in writing to give its consent within eight days from the day on which the employer asks for it. The dismissal of the worker council member or trade union representative without the trade union's consent is invalid. However, the employer may claim in court that such dismissal is valid even without the trade union's consent if all other prerequisites for termination are satisfied and it would be unjust to require that the employer continue to employ such trade union officer. If the employee council/trade union representative does not provide any response, it is considered that he/she agrees with the decision. The statement of refusal of the workers union/trade union representative must be in writing and include reasoning. The employer has the right to claim that the statement of refusal is replaced by a court or arbitration judgment.

If the employer wishes to dismiss an employee who is not a worker council member or trade union representative, it may do so without the trade union's consent. However, the employer must discuss each notice or immediate cancellation with the employee council before the notice or immediate cancellation is served. A breach of this obligation may render the dismissal invalid but may result in a fine of up to EUR7 960) being imposed on the employer by the Work Inspectorate.

20.6.6 Severance Payment

[402] If employment is terminated by notice given by the employer for reasons cited under paragraph **[398] (iii) (a) and (b),** the employee is entitled to a severance payment which is determined according to the duration of employment with the employer. The minimum amount of the severance payment is one-third of the average monthly salary (last three months), for each year of work with the employer. The maximum amount of the severance payment is six monthly salaries, achieved in the last three-month period. The employer may grant a higher severance payment to its employees under either collective bargaining agreements, or the employer's internal regulations, or under an individual contract.

[403] If employment is terminated by notice given by the employer for a reason cited under paragraph **[398] (iii) (c)**, [399] or by agreement for the same reason, the employee is entitled to a severance payment in the amount of twelve months' average salary.

20.7 Employment Representatives

[404] Employees can form either trade unions or work councils as their representatives in employment relations. Alternatively, they may not be represented, in which case the employer must fulfil certain duties (e.g., the duty to inform) towards all employees directly.

20.7.1 Trade Unions

Basic Principles

[405] The basic principles under which trade unions operate in Croatia are the following: (i) trade unions can be established irrespective of the will of the employer and must be registered as a trade union; (ii) they represent all the employees of a particular employer, irrespective of their will to be so represented and of their membership in the union; and (iii) it is forbidden to ban the trade union or to dissolve it by a decision of the executive branch of government; and (iv) no one can be treated more favourably or unfavourably because of his membership or involvement in the trade union.

Establishing a Trade Union

[406] A trade union may be established by at least ten adults with legal capacity. The trade union has articles of association whose content is prescribed by the Labour Act. A trade union becomes a legal entity upon its registration with the relevant entity competent for registering associations (the Ministry of Administration and Justice). The court does not decide on the establishment of a trade union. It simply registers its existence, provided that all the required documents are submitted. Upon its registration with the registration entity, the trade union is established and assumes all the authority granted to it by legal rules and regulations.

[407] Trade unions operate at company level, but can also join with other trade unions of higher level, which operate nation-wide.

20.7.2 Employee Councils

[408] An employer with a minimum of twenty employees is eligible for the establishment of an employee council. The employee council is elected on free elections by secret vote. The number of employee council members depends on the number of employees employed by the employer, that is:

Employees	*Employee Council Members*
Up to 75	1
75–250	3

Employees	*Employee Council Members*
251–500	5
501–750	7
751–1000	9
For each next 1 000 threshold	+2 employees

The employee council may coexist together with a trade union of an employer.

[409] The employer is obliged to organize elections to the employee council upon the petition of the trade union or at least 20% of the employees. The employee council is duly elected only if at least one-third of the employees participate in the elections. The term of office is four years. Employee councils always operate within a single employer.

[410] An employee council operates as a mediator between the employer and the employees. Its powers are less extensive than those of a trade union. The employee council represents the employees in the exercise of their right to obtain information and their right of negotiation. Employee councils are not legal entities (i.e., they do not have any legal capacity). Also, employee councils do not have a right to collective bargaining or to execute collective agreements, and may not, therefore, employ extreme measures, such as strikes, to resolve collective disputes.

20.7.3 Role of Employee Representatives

[411] The Labour Act provides that one member of the management board or supervisory board of the employer shall be an employee representative. He is elected by the employee council.

20.7.4 Collective Bargaining/Collective Agreements

[412] Trade unions are the exclusive representatives of the employees in collective bargaining and in the conclusion of collective bargaining agreements, regardless of whether those employees are members of a trade union. The trade union bodies execute these agreements on behalf of all employees, at the company level (company collective bargaining agreements) or at the industry level (so-called higher-level collective bargaining agreements).

[413] Higher-level collective bargaining agreements are binding on all employees and employers in the industry/business in question.

[414] If several trade unions operate side by side at an employer, the employer must negotiate the collective agreement with all such trade unions.

[415] The procedural regulations governing collective bargaining, are contained in the Labour Act, while criteria for representativeness of trade unions and employer associations for collective bargaining is regulated within the Act on Representativeness of Employers' Associations and Trade Unions. However, the Labour Act primarily regulates types of collective bargaining agreements which exist (both in-company and higher-level – i.e., those concluded between employer organizations and higher trade union bodies), including the resolution of collective disputes, if any (including strikes). A procedure is provided for collective bargaining, in particular for its commencement, such that collective bargaining is commenced upon the submission by either party to the other party of a written proposal for the conclusion of a collective bargaining agreement.

20.7.5 Obligation to inform

[416] Employers must provide certain information to the employee council or employee representative bodies (e.g., information on the likely development of the business situation, its effect on the socio-economic status of the employees, the status of the organization, occupational health and safety matters, changes in work organization). The employer is obliged to provide this information every three months.

[417] The 'right to obtain information' means the provision of the necessary data from which the state of communicated fact can be explicitly ascertained and if relevant, an opinion regarding this fact can be formed. The employer must provide this information sufficiently far in advance and in a suitable manner in order that the employees can consider it and prepare for the consultation process with the employer.

[418] If a trade union is active within a company, the employer must provide even more information to the trade union. The employer is obliged to inform the relevant trade union of, for example, any expected changes in the level of wages/ salaries, the average wage, the company's economic and financial situation, and the work conditions and structure of the workforce. The employer's power to decide at its own discretion remains unaffected by its obligation to provide information.

20.7.6 Right of Consultation

[419] The employer is obliged to submit certain issues to the trade union representative and to the employee council for negotiation before deciding on such issues. The right to decide on any issue remains exclusively with the employer. However, failure to conduct the consultation process with the employee council renders any decision invalid and without effect and the employer may be fined by the competent inspectorate by a monetary fine up to EUR7.960 00.

[420] The right of consultation means consultations between the employer and the employees and the exchange of views and explanations with the objective of reaching an agreement. The undertaking must arrange for a consultation to take place sufficiently far in advance and in an appropriate manner so that the employees can express their views on the basis of the information supplied so that these views might be properly considered before the measure is implemented by the employer. The employees have the right to be provided with a reasoned response to their views. Before the implementation of the measure in question, the employees have the right to demand sufficient information and explanations. The employees also have the right to demand personal negotiations at the appropriate management level, depending on the nature of the matter. The employer, employees and the employee representatives are obliged to cooperate and to proceed in line with their justified interests.

[421] The Labour Act provides a model/exemplary list of those matters that the employer is obliged to negotiate with the trade union body. The employer is obliged to negotiate, for example, salaries, new hirings and terminations, annual leave plan, technological updates in work process, transfer of business activity and transfer of employment agreements to another employer. If the employee council does not respond within eight days, it is presumed to have agreed with the intended decision, and any objections and comments have to be explained and given in writing.

20.7.7 Right to Decide Jointly

[422] Another power enjoyed by the trade unions is the right to decide jointly with the employer on certain matters, which are terminations to specific categories of employees. The Croatian Labour Act provides an exhaustive list of these cases.

[423] Joint decision-making means that certain measures proposed by the employer may only be introduced with the prior consent of the relevant trade union representative or employee council. If the employer fails to receive such prior consent, then its decisions are invalid.

[424] The most important issues in respect of which the employer must obtain the prior consent of the trade union is the termination (including the immediate termination) of the employment of an employee who is a trade union officer (during his/her term of office and one year thereafter), unless such employee agrees to the termination.

20.7.8 Right to Decide

[425] Trade unions decide independently on, for example, matters related to their establishment, internal structure, activities, assets, membership fees, and the possible employment of employees for their own needs. A trade union acts as an employer towards its employees and provides them with remuneration.

20.8 Particular Aspects Related to Acquisitions

20.8.1 Share Transaction

[426] If an acquisition is structured as a share transaction, the identity of the employer remains unchanged. A share deal will not affect the existing employment or any of the mutual rights and duties under existing employment contracts.

In a share transaction, in general, a trade union active within the employer has no co-decision or supervision rights in relation to the transaction, and the employer has no duty to inform the trade union (or any other employee representatives) about the transaction, unless it would affect employees.

20.8.2 Asset Transaction

[427] A different regime applies to an asset transaction in which the employer changes as a result of the transaction. In such case, all employment contracts pertaining to the acquired business transfer to the purchaser by operation of law, and no modification to the employment contract is required. An asset deal as such does not trigger the transfer of employment. Rather, this happens only if the original employer's activities are transferred.

The Croatian Labour Act stipulates that if an enterprise or a part thereof is transferred to a new owner, all employments which existed at the time of the transfer and pertaining to the enterprise, or to the part transferred shall pass to the new owner by operation of law.

If an enterprise or a part thereof or some of the employer's activities are transferred to another employer, all rights and obligations arising from the employment or affected employees are transferred to the new employer. The original employer's rights and obligations towards employees whose employment was terminated before the day of the transfer remain unchanged.

The employer is obligated to consult on the intended transfer with the employee council. If there are no such employee representative bodies, the employer must inform the employees affected by the transfer about the transfer directly. Although the consultation with employee council must take place, it does not affect the final decision of the employer.

The employees cannot prevent themselves being transferred to a new employer, i.e., their only option is to terminate their employment agreement.

20.9 Employment of Foreigners in Croatia

[428] All foreigners (except citizens of the Member States of European Union, the European Economic Area and Switzerland, including their family members) without permanent residence in Croatia must obtain a relevant permit in order to be allowed to stay and work in Croatia.

20.9.1 Employment by Local Entity

[429] If a foreigner is coming to Croatia to become an employee of a Croatian employer, such employment is possible only if the employer has notified Croatian citizens of such work vacancy and if the employee has obtained a so-called work and stay permit, which serves both as a work and residency permit. An employee may apply for a work and stay permit at the Ministry of Internal Affairs. The intention of the authorities is that the whole process should take approximately four weeks; however, usually it takes longer. For some employment positions, it is necessary to conduct a test of the labour market. This test is conducted by the Croatian Employment Bureau to determine whether any Croatian citizens (unemployed) are available for that position for which the foreign employee is employed. If there are no available unemployed citizens, a positive opinion is issued by the Bureau. This positive opinion may be a prerequisite for obtaining the work and stay permit.

20.9.2 Secondment of an Employee to Croatia

[430] If a foreigner is seconded by a foreign employer to work temporarily at a Croatian employer which is a connected entity, such secondment is possible only if the employee has obtained: (i) a work and stay permit issued by the Ministry of Internal Affairs. The work permit must be applied for in close cooperation with the local employer. The whole process should take about three to four weeks, however, usually it takes longer.

21 INTELLECTUAL PROPERTY RIGHTS

[431] Intellectual property rights recognized under Croatian law can be broadly divided into two groups. Copyright (and related rights) covers artistic and creative works, while industrial property rights protect knowledge with an industrial application.

21.1 Copyright

[432] Copyright and its related rights are regulated primarily by the Copyright Act (Official Gazette No. 111/21, the 'Copyright Act'). The Copyright Act regulates the following types of rights:

(i) copyright of the author to Copyrighted Works (as defined below); and
(ii) related rights.

21.1.1 Copyrighted Works

[433] A Copyright work is an original intellectual creation within the literary, scientific or artistic field that has an individual character, regardless of the manner and form of expression, type, value or purpose, unless otherwise determined by this Copyright Act (e.g., musical works, dramatic and dramatic-musical works, choreographic and pantomime works, audiovisual works, video games).

[434] Ideas, procedures, work methods or mathematical concepts as such are not protected under the Copyright Act but their expressions are. The following are also not considered as copyrighted works discoveries, ideas, and principles on which any element of a computer program is based, including those on which its interfaces are based, and daily news and other news having the character of ordinary media information. Furthermore, no protection is extended to public works (e.g., legislation, court decisions or public documents). Folk literary and artistic creations in their original form are not subject to copyright, but for their communication to the public a fee is paid.

21.1.2 Authorship

[435] The author of a copyright work is a natural person who created the work. The author gains copyright over his work by creating the work. No registration is possible or necessary. The author is considered to be a natural person whose name, pseudonym, artistic sign or code is indicated in the usual way on copies of the author's work or when the author's work is published, until the contrary is proven.

[436] If two or more authors compile their created works for the purpose of their joint use, each of the authors retains the copyright on their work. Mutual relations between the authors of compiled works are governed by an agreement. If such agreement has not been concluded it is considered that all authors of the compiled work have the right to an equal share of the compensation for use of the compiled work. Co-authors of a copyright work are persons who jointly created the work, whose contributions cannot be used independently. Co-authors have a joint copyright on the created work, so that each of them has a part of that copyright calculated proportionally to the entire copyright.

21.1.3 Author's rights

[437] The author of any Copyrighted Work has moral and economic rights.

Moral rights of the author include the right to: (i) first publication; (ii) claim authorship; (iii) respect the author's work; (iv) respect the honour and reputation of the author; and (v) a revocation right. Please note that the moral rights of the author are inalienable and may not be waived.

The economic rights of the author extend to the usage (i.e., reproduction right, distribution right, right of public communication, and processing right) of the Copyrighted Work by the author. The author has the right to an appropriate and proportionate renumeration for any use of copyright work. The author may grant a licence to a third person to use Copyrighted Work.

[438] Copyright cannot be subject to enforcement and is not transferable (except inheritance). Economic gains derived from the use of Copyright can be subject to enforcement. Also, the author may transfer one or more of his economic rights to another person.

[439] There are some cases when the rights of the author are limited by operation of law (e.g., where an employer is exercising any and all economic rights of its employees unless otherwise agreed).

21.1.4 Protection and Enforcement of Copyright

[440] The author may protect and enforce copyright via the courts if there has been an infringement of his right or in the event of an impending infringement of his rights.

[441] The author may request from the person who violated his right, or his general successor, the cessation of the action that violates that right and the omission of such or similar actions in the future, reparation of the damages, payment of compensation for unauthorized use, payment of a penalty specified by law, return or compensation of all benefits acquired without grounds, the determination of the committed violation, as well as the publication of the final judgment by which the court, even partially, complied with the request aimed at protecting the author's rights. In addition to the author, persons who acquired a derived right from copyright or related rights, and in accordance with the content and nature of that derived right, have the right to appropriate protection.

[442] The Copyright Act also provides for the creation of collective rights management organizations, which may assist authors with the protection and enforcement of their copyright. Membership of such organizations is generally voluntary; however, the collective rights organizations are exclusively responsible for the collection and distribution of certain types of royalties.

21.1.5 Due Diligence Verification

[443] Since it is not possible to register copyright in Croatia, its verification during any due diligence must be made on an individual basis.

[444] Wherever the use of copyright is identified, the relevant company should be able to demonstrate its right to use such copyright, either by virtue of authorship or of a license. Please note in this context that license agreements have to be in writing.

[445] A particular issue encountered in M&A transactions is whether a company holds or is entitled to use economic rights on copyrighted work made by the company's employees. In this respect please note that the employee is still considered as an author and relations about the author's work created in the employment relationship are regulated by the Copyright Act, the employment agreement or by some other act regulating the employment relationship or by some other agreement concluded between the author and the employer.

22 INDUSTRIAL PROPERTY RIGHTS

[446] Industrial property rights refer to: (i) patents; (ii) geographical indications; (iii) industrial designs; (iv) trademarks; and (v) topographies of semiconductor products.

22.1 Registration of Industrial Property Rights

[447] All industrial property rights have in common the fact that they are only created by their registration with the State Intellectual Property Office (the DZIV). For the purposes of such registration, potential rights holders must complete a form (which is available on the DZIV's website), attach to it the required additional documentation, and submit it to the DZIV. Furthermore, a registration fee of approximately EUR20–500 (depending on the type of industrial property right being registered) must be paid by the applicant.

[448] During the registration proceedings, DZIV verifies whether the basic legal conditions for registration are met. With respect to the individual types of industrial properties, these conditions could be summarized in the following manner:

(i) patents – novelty in relation to the existing technological state, inventive step/level (i.e., non-obvious to one familiar with the relevant technical field) and industrial applicability (i.e., practical applicability on an industrial scale); in particular, scientific theories, mathematical methods, business processes, software, medical processes and therapeutic methods are not patentable;
(ii) geographical indications – a specific form of protection, which necessarily implies the essential or exclusive influence of special natural and human factors of a certain geographical environment and the resulting special quality and properties of products or services. In such a case it is necessary for the production, preparation and processing of products and services to take place entirely in the indicated area.
(iii) industrial designs – such designs (i.e., the visual look of a product) may be registered if the relevant design is new and has an individualized nature;
(iv) trademarks – any designation (words, pictures, numbers, colours, shapes, packaging) must enable the clear differentiation of a certain person's products or services from another person's products or services of the same kind; furthermore, a trade mark will not be registered if it is identical or similar to an existing trade mark in such a way that could be misleading to the public, provided an owner of the existing trademark files an objection to the registration of the new trademark with the DZIV;
(v) topographies of semiconductor products – topographies may be registered if they are the result of the creative activity of their author and if they are not common in the semiconductor industry.

22.2 Protection and Enforcement of Industrial Property Rights

[449] The rights of the creators of industrial property rights mostly extend to the use of their industrial property (i.e., to the production of products incorporating such industrial property and to the granting of a licence to do so to third parties). The rights holders may also fully or partially transfer their industrial property rights to third parties.

[450] Holders of industrial property rights have the following rights:

(i) a creator of industrial property rights or his legal successor can claim the determination of creator's right to protect industrial right against a person who has filed an application for registration of industrial right without authorization;
(ii) to request that a court determines any infringement of industrial right and to request a 'cease and desist' order and the elimination of the consequences of the infringement (e.g., by means of the recall of unauthorized products from the market and/or the destruction of any unauthorized products or tools used for the creation of unauthorized products); and
(iii) compensation of damages, unjust enrichment and non-material loss (this may take the form of monetary compensation or publishing of a judgment).

The above-mentioned claims may also be brought by a licensee.

22.3 Due Diligence Verification

[451] Since all industrial property rights must be registered with the DZIV, verification for due diligence purposes is relatively straightforward, as the registers of the DZIV are searchable online.

[452] Please note that transfers of industrial rights should also be registered with the DZIV. While a failure to register a transfer with the DZIV does not render such a transfer invalid, such a transfer would not be effective against third parties (e.g., any claims for infringement would have to be brought by the original rights holder). Similarly, licences only become effective against third parties by their registration with the IPO (this is relevant in particular with respect to exclusive licences).

23 ACCOUNTING TREATMENT

23.1 General

[453] The format and content of group accounts is determined by Croatian Accounting Act.

[454] Large enterprises and enterprises of public interest must prepare their accounts in accordance with International Financial Reporting Standards (IFRS).

[455] Micro, small, and medium enterprises that are not listed as public interest entities must prepare their accounts in accordance with Croatian Financial Reporting Standards (HFRS).

23.2 Merger, Demerger, Squeeze-Out

[456] Merging or demerging companies must file financial reports and a tax return to the Tax Administration with the date preceding the date of the merger or division. They must close their business accounts with that date as well.

23.3 Transformation of the Legal Form

[457] In general, in case of transformation of the legal form, the company need not close their books. From that point of view, transformation is neutral.

23.4 Other Issues

[458] In terms of accounting, mergers are treated using the purchase, i.e., acquisition method, which is based on the assumption that the company acquires the net assets of one or more companies through the merger. That method requires the following analysis:

(1) Defining the acquirer. An acquirer is generally defined as a company that acquires control over another merging company, applying the requirements of HSFI 2 and IFRS 10 – Consolidated Financial Statements.
(2) Defining the acquisition date: the date on which the acquirer acquired control over the acquiree.
(3) The determination of the value of assets, assumed liabilities and possible non-controlling interests in the acquired entity.
(4) Determination of the value of goodwill or profit purchase gain. In doing so, goodwill is recognized as the difference between the total amount of the transferred acquisition consideration, any non-controlling interest and the net amount of the ascertainable acquired assets and assumed liabilities, the value of which is determined in accordance with the requirements of IFRS 3 and HSFI 2.

www.ingramcontent.com/pod-product-compliance
Lightning Source LLC
Chambersburg PA
CBHW071352230926
51846CB00002B/528
9789403500379